Communication Skills

Master the Art of Analyzing People, Talk to Anyone with Confidence, and Instantly Boost Your Social Intelligence

© Copyright 2023 - All rights reserved.

The content contained within this book may not be reproduced, duplicated, or transmitted without direct written permission from the author or the publisher.

Under no circumstances will any blame or legal responsibility be held against the publisher, or author, for any damages, reparation, or monetary loss due to the information contained within this book, either directly or indirectly.

Legal Notice:

This book is copyright protected. It is only for personal use. You cannot amend, distribute, sell, use, quote or paraphrase any part, or the content within this book, without the consent of the author or publisher.

Disclaimer Notice:

Please note the information contained within this document is for educational and entertainment purposes only. All effort has been executed to present accurate, up-to-date, reliable, and complete information. No warranties of any kind are declared or implied. Readers acknowledge that the author is not engaging in the rendering of legal, financial, medical, or professional advice. The content within this book has been derived from various sources. Please consult a licensed professional before attempting any techniques outlined in this book.

By reading this document, the reader agrees that under no circumstances is the author responsible for any losses, direct or indirect, that are incurred as a result of the use of the information contained within this document, including, but not limited to, errors, omissions, or inaccuracies.

Free Bonus from Andy Gardner

Hi!

My name is Andy Gardner, and first off, I want to THANK YOU for reading my book.

Now you have a chance to join my exclusive email list related to human psychology and self-development so you can get the ebook below for free as well as the potential to get more ebooks for free! Simply click the link below to join.

P.S. Remember that it's 100% free to join the list.

Access your free bonuses here:
https://livetolearn.lpages.co/andy-gardner-communication-skills-paperback/

Table of Contents

PART 1: COMMUNICATION SKILLS TRAINING 1
- INTRODUCTION 2
- CHAPTER 1: THE WHY BEHIND COMMUNICATION SKILLS 4
- CHAPTER 2: HOW TO TRULY LISTEN 14
- CHAPTER 3: 5 WAYS TO HEAR THE EMOTIONS BEHIND THE WORDS 24
- CHAPTER 4: HOW BODY LANGUAGE CAN MAKE OR BREAK A CONVERSATION 34
- CHAPTER 5: HOW TO SPARK UP A CONVERSATION WITH ANYONE 45
- CHAPTER 6: INSTANTLY MASTER THE ART OF STORYTELLING 57
- CHAPTER 7: 15 TIPS TO COMMUNICATE IN GROUPS EFFORTLESSLY 66
- CHAPTER 8: BECOME AN AMAZING PUBLIC SPEAKER 75
- CHAPTER 9: HOW TO MANAGE AN ARGUMENT LIKE A BOSS 84
- CHAPTER 10: 23 STRATEGIES TO END A CONVERSATION SMOOTHLY 93
- CONCLUSION 102

PART 2: HOW TO ANALYZE PEOPLE 104
- INTRODUCTION 105
- CHAPTER 1: WHAT CAN HUMAN BEHAVIOR TELL US? 107
- CHAPTER 2: THE HISTORY OF HUMAN BEHAVIOR ANALYSIS 113
- CHAPTER 3: DECODING SOMEONE'S VERBAL BEHAVIOR 121
- CHAPTER 4: PICKING UP ON NON-VERBAL CUES 129
- CHAPTER 5: UNDERSTANDING DIFFERENT PERSONALITY TYPES 141
- CHAPTER 6: THE WHY BEHIND LIES 163
- CHAPTER 7: IDENTIFYING DECEPTION IN PEOPLE 173
- CHAPTER 8: TRUTH INDICATORS IN LIES 182
- CHAPTER 9: HOW TO READ PEOPLE LIKE A BOOK 191
- BONUS: ANALYZING PEOPLE'S CHEAT SHEET 200
- CONCLUSION 210

HERE'S ANOTHER BOOK BY ANDY GARDNER THAT YOU MIGHT LIKE 212
FREE BONUS FROM ANDY GARDNER 213
REFERENCES 214

Part 1: Communication Skills Training

How to Talk to Anyone about Anything and Immediately Improve Your Social Intelligence, Active Listening Skills, and Public Speaking

Introduction

What if we all had the same speaking tones, body language, and facial expressions? Imagine that nothing in how we speak changed, regardless of the situation or message we're trying to deliver. It would be tough to understand what anyone was trying to say, right?

A simple phrase, such as "Well done!" can be used in either a cheerful or sarcastic context. "That's it!" can either mean "stop" or "Yes, what you're doing is right! Keep it up." Putting something into words is not enough. You can never know what a person truly means if they don't try to communicate it to you. Communication is a two-way street. Communication skills are a person's ability to deliver a message effectively via numerous tools, including tone, context, body language, facial expression, active listening, and being straightforward.

Being a great communicator is an indispensable life skill. It is crucial to the success of your career, achieving your personal goals, and maintaining healthy relationships. While some people are born communicators, others struggle to communicate their messages, get tongue-tied, and mumble. The good news is that you can learn and develop the ability to communicate effectively, just like any other skill.

We don't only use our communication skills when we need to convey an idea or express our feelings. These skills are also used whenever we receive any kind of information. This is because a large part of our communication skills depends on our ability to listen, observe, process, empathize, and react. Excellent communicators are aware of other people's styles of interaction through observing communication on different mediums, understanding that those styles vary depending on the place, environment, and means of interaction. Some people express their emotions more effectively through phone conversations than physical interactions. Other people are better at communicating via text, although this form of communication is always subject to misunderstandings. You may find it hard to speak your mind in public, but you easily share your ideas in private spaces.

Excellent communication skills guarantee that everyone will understand you and that you understand them too. Good communicators are generally self-assured and confident. Not worrying about misinterpreted conversations takes a significant load off your shoulders.

Reading this book will give you a greater understanding of why communication skills are highly valued, especially in today's world. You'll learn about the different skills and their characteristics, how to be an active listener, and how to hear the emotions behind people's words. You'll learn how mastering body language is the key to maintaining an engaging conversation.

The best thing about this book is that it offers practical information on how to start a conversation with anyone, even if you're an introvert. It offers numerous strategies to help you initiate conversations with others while leaving great first impressions. You'll also learn how to master the art of storytelling, so you can keep people interested and engaged. Then, you'll come across step-by-step instructions showing you how to manage arguments and end conversations without feeling awkward.

Chapter 1: The Why behind Communication Skills

In this chapter, you'll learn everything you need to know about why you need to develop your communication skills. You'll learn the benefits of being a good communicator and understand the different types of communication you can use. Finally, you'll read about the different styles and how they can be used daily.

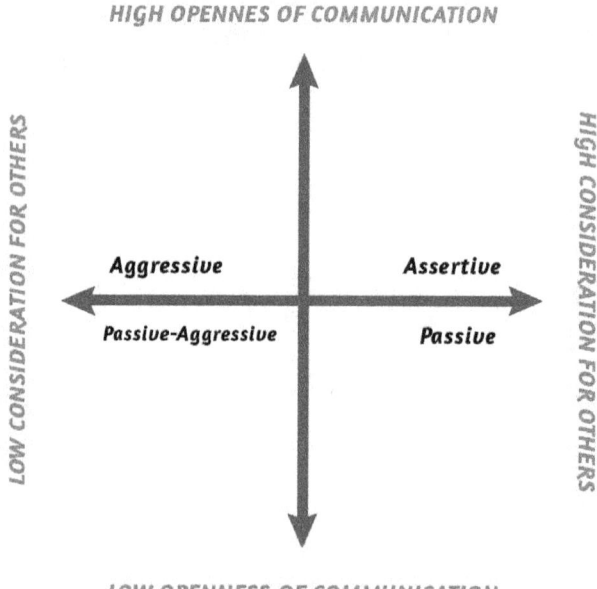

The Benefits of Having Excellent Communication Skills

Having good communication skills is an invaluable asset in both personal and professional settings. The ability to be understood and understand others depends on cultivating mutual trust and respect, which are essentially the foundation of all healthy relationships. Communicating effectively with others helps you build up and maintain strong relationships. Lacking this skill can drive a wedge between you and those around you. Speaking your mind and expressing yourself eloquently allows you to cultivate and maintain good social, romantic, familial, and professional relationships.

People with excellent communication skills are generally more confident and assured. If you're worried about not getting your message through to your audience, you could be seen as hesitant and full of self-doubt. This is a compelling reason people with great communication skills receive more job offers than the average person. They never sell themselves short! Since most disagreements arise from misunderstandings or refusal to tolerate an opposing point of view, excellent communicators are rarely subject to conflict.

Great ideas mean nothing if they are not appropriately communicated. Imagine how many great inventions never made it because their creators were inarticulate and failed to pitch them compellingly.

The benefits of having good communication skills are countless. Here are a few things that being a good communicator can do for you:

Creates a Healthy Work Environment

You can create a healthy work environment for yourself and others by learning to communicate effectively. Trust is the most critical factor in positive workplaces. Coworkers who don't trust each other won't work well together and will always be in competition. While some competition is needed to maintain a productive and exciting work environment, too much competition can lead to discord, a lack of unity, and unhappy organization-client relationships. This is because employees start prioritizing personal goals and lose sight of the bigger picture.

When you nurture a sense of trust between you and your coworkers, you'll be able to promote positive attitudes and stronger relationships. This can relieve some of the tension and stress which occurs in the workplace, which can reduce misunderstandings.

Helps You Succeed in Your Career Path

Excellent communication skills can help you succeed in your career path, regardless of your industry. Whether you communicate directly with clients, report to your manager, participate in group projects or oversee a team, your success largely depends on your ability to communicate effectively. While each job comes with different structures, challenges, and communication dynamics, the skills you need to excel in this area are universal.

It helps to observe how everyone around you interacts so you can start mimicking and building on these insights. Not only will this help you develop your skills, but it also allows you to understand others which can help you diffuse conflicts and become a better negotiator.

Makes You Appear Charismatic and Attractive

There's a thin line between knowing how to communicate and being an effective communicator. Like all other skills, you must continue nurturing and developing your communication skills. If you don't continue learning, you'll lose your capacity to communicate your message effectively.

How you communicate with others is an entire process that begins the moment you enter the room. How you carry and present yourself and the first impression you make all count toward your communication skill set. Imagine you're a salesman meeting up with a client to sell them a luxurious watch. How will your client respond to your effort? Even if you build up an extraordinary pitch, if you walk in with a slouchy posture in sweatpants and start stumbling over your words, your communication will be less effective. They'll likely turn down your offer. Your appearance and attitude play a part in your overall message.

How you look and behave must be relevant to whatever you're trying to communicate. You should also be able to appeal to the person you're dealing with and capture their imagination. We often forget that most of our conversations are about the people we're talking to and not about ourselves. Even if you're recounting a particular event in your life, your sentence structure, vocabulary, and what you choose to tell or leave out all depend on who you're talking to. Try to figure out as much as you can about the person's personality, beliefs, and interests so you can appeal to them and address them appropriately. Learn to respect other people's opinions even when they don't align with your own, and practice active listening. This makes it easier to get along with others.

Improves Your Problem-Solving Skills

Having good problem-solving skills enriches your personal and professional life. If you're filling a managerial position, you probably already know this skill is essential if you are a team leader or manager. It also makes you more adaptable to change and allows you to quickly deal with conflicts. Problem-solvers can handle unexpected situations without being held back by fear and anxiety. Those with good communication skills are active listeners and can empathize with others. They know which questions to ask to find the answers they're searching for. Good communicators can tell when they can step in to help someone or listen to them and when to let them sort things out independently. They know exactly what to say to people whenever they're struggling.

Allows You to Feel Better about Yourself

How you communicate with others determines how much you can connect with them. You can't get to know someone intimately if you don't know how to communicate well with them. Being an excellent communicator requires you to be an honest and authentic speaker. Communicating in a genuine way that aligns with who you truly are will make you feel good about yourself.

Offers a Sense of Direction and Clarity

People only know what to expect of you, whether at work or in your personal life, if you can communicate your plans, objectives, and wishes to them. They also know what you expect of them in a friendship, romantic relationship, or as a team member at work. This sense of clarity is critical at work because it helps you and your team identify problems whenever something isn't heading in the right direction. Developing communication skills also teaches you to effectively deliver constructive feedback, which is needed to steer things onto the right track. Setting clear expectations for those in your life can help you maintain healthy relationships, ensure no one crosses your boundaries, and avoid conflicts. It enables you to determine when your efforts aren't being reciprocated and allows you to communicate exactly how you feel.

Fosters Better Relationships

Communication is vital when it comes to any relationship. Communicating your interests, thoughts, needs, desires, feelings, and emotions and actively listening to those of others is essential to the maintenance of healthy relationships. You must also be able to speak up if they hurt you so that you can work together toward a resolution. Some people prefer to let hurtful situations slide. However, they don't realize that they're slowly accumulating all their friend's or partners' faults, which eventually leads to resentment. It's essential to be able to talk about anything with those who are closest to you. Otherwise, undesirable feelings, which will ultimately ruin the relationship, will arise.

Keeps You Engaged

Good communication skills come with better comprehension and confidence. When you know exactly what you need to do and grow confident in your abilities, you become more engaged at work and in your passions and hobbies. If you're a manager, communicating with your employees can increase their job satisfaction and make them feel more engaged.

Enhances Productivity

Communicating with your employees or coworkers lets you understand each other's roles and expectations. When everything is clearly communicated from the beginning, everyone can focus on doing their work instead of wasting time on things that don't matter. This applies to every part of life. For instance, talking to your partner about your plans and to-do list, and asking them to wash the dishes, instead of waiting for you to come back home would be a lot more effective than complaining about having so much on your plate and expecting them to help out on their own initiative. The latter situation would result in an easily avoidable argument and leave you with additional chores.

How Effective Communication Changed Ian's Life

This is what Ian told us about his life:

> *"I wasn't always great at communicating with others, particularly when it came to my needs, expectations, and feelings. I expected everyone to know what I expected from them without uttering a single word about it. I expected them to know how to deal with me when I was feeling down, when to leave me alone, and when to try to get me to talk. I thought they already knew how I like to be joked around with - what was acceptable for me and what wasn't. I expected everyone to stick to their boundaries and mine, even though I'd never communicated them.*

Guess what I did when my expectations weren't met. I felt uncomfortable with someone's jokes or banter, or when someone crossed my boundaries. I gave them the cold shoulder until I felt like talking to them again. I didn't bother to explain why I distanced myself from anyone, which left them confused. The more someone repeated their "mistakes" (or actions that they had no idea bothered me at all), the colder and more distant I grew. This sounds very toxic, doesn't it?

I knew that the way I was behaving was wrong, but I didn't have the energy or the know-how to remedy the situation. It was easier to let people go or figure things out on their own than to try to communicate with them. It wasn't until I started to lose people who meant the world to me that I realized that I had to do something.

This is when I decided to learn how to start communicating. In the beginning, it was very hard for me to start telling people that they hurt me when they did this or that or that it bothered me when someone joked about one of my insecurities. I worried that I'd come off as uptight if I listed my boundaries or said that I didn't like it when someone disrespected or made fun of me, even as a joke. However, I knew that it was unfair to everyone around me.

Communicating with others didn't make me appear vulnerable or defensive like I thought it would. If anything, people started trusting and respecting me more. They no longer walked on eggshells around me, and I noticed that my relationships grew significantly stronger. I no longer felt horrible for treating my loved ones the way I did. I never admitted the fact that I knew that they deserved better."

Types of Communication

There are several types of communication. However, the following seven are the most popular ones:

Verbal Communication

Verbal communication is the chief method of communication. We all use it to communicate and deliver our messages to others.

Verbal communication is broken down into oral and written communication. Face-to-face or phone conversations are examples of the former, while a written letter or text message is an example of written communication.

Non-Verbal Communication

This is a subtler type of communication, and it encompasses any form of communication that is non-verbal and not written. This includes body language, posture, gestures, eye contact, and facial expressions. People underestimate the expressive effectiveness of being able to communicate without saying much. Most of our emotions are conveyed through this skill.

Watch any movie you've never seen before. Turn the volume and any subtitles off. You'll probably be able to tell whether the character is happy, sad, angry, neutral, or surprised just by observing their facial reactions, hand gestures, and body language.

Written Communication

Written communication is a subtype of verbal communication and refers to expressing oneself using written words. Blogs, articles, emails, text messages, and letters are all types of written communication.

Oral Communication

This is another subtype of verbal communication, and it refers to interacting via spoken word. TV reporters, talk shows, face-to-face conversations, speeches, seminars, lectures, and phone calls are all examples of oral communication. This is considered the best communication skill that anyone can master because you can tweak your language and tone of voice to deliver the desired emotion along with your message.

Active Listening

Many people don't know that active listening is a communication skill. It is one of the most important, for that matter. Active listening requires you to mindfully listen to others and take the time to process and reflect on their words. You must be attentive to the speaker's thoughts, emotions, and feelings.

Visual Communication

Visual communication refers to the expression of thoughts and feelings through visual media. The pictures you come across on blogs are examples of visual communication. Videos, stickers, and gifs are all examples of visual communication. Our activities on social media platforms like Instagram and Snapchat rely on this form of communication.

Mass Communication

This type of communication refers to sharing information with a large audience, such as via newspapers or TV. Like verbal communication, this skill comes in oral and written forms.

Communication Styles

There are four different communication styles - how people communicate, which is different for everyone. However, there are four main styles, and if you can identify them, you'll be able to navigate the minefield that mixed messages can leave in their wake, such as misunderstandings, misinterpretations, and arguments. Understanding the different communication styles can help you interact with different people more effectively.

Passive Communication Style

These types of communicators like to avoid the spotlight. They are generally quiet and are often indifferent during arguments and debates. They seldom take a stand or show any assertive behavior. Passive individuals don't talk about their feelings or needs, which is why you'll struggle to determine whether or not they're feeling uncomfortable or need guidance.

Here are some signs you're dealing with a passive communicator:

- They can't say "no."
- They have a soft voice
- They are generally apologetic
- They avoid making eye contact
- They're easy-going
- They have a poor posture
- They fidget often

When dealing with passive communicators, it's best to be straightforward and initiate private conversations. Ask for their input and opinions to make them feel involved, and avoid asking "yes" or "no" questions.

You must start developing your communication skills if you're a passive communicator. Seize the opportunity to speak up whenever you can do so comfortably. Experiment with written communications until you ease into oral ones.

Aggressive Communication Style

These communicators allow their thoughts and feelings to get in the way. They behave and speak impulsively without thinking about their actions all the way through. This compromises their social and professional relationships and decreases their productivity at work.

The following are some signs of aggressive communicators:

- They interrupt others while they're speaking
- They have an overbearing posture
- They maintain firm eye contact
- They usually invade other people's personal spaces

You need to approach an aggressive communicator calmly while maintaining your assertiveness. If they're your coworker, avoid discussing their feelings or personal issues by keeping the conversation strictly professional. You need to know when to walk away from this individual, so you don't risk wasting your time or getting into an argument.

If you're an aggressive communicator, you need to work on introducing positive communication techniques into your life. It will also help to reduce stress levels.

Passive-Aggressive Communication Style

Passive-aggressive communicators approach situations aggressively – especially people driven by passion and motivation while appearing passive on the outside. While so the language they use is calm and sweet, their actions are the complete opposite. These individuals are excellent manipulators- they steer everything in a direction that only benefits them.

Passive-aggressive individuals often:

- Behave sarcastically
- Exhibit denial tendencies
- Look happy even though they're feeling down
- Mutter
- Resort to the silent treatment

Make straightforward requests when dealing with this type of person, so you leave no room for confusion or debate. Always make sure you confront their unacceptable behavior. Get their honest opinion by asking for their feedback.

If you have this communication style, practice communicating your thoughts and feelings with others.

Assertive

This is the most productive communication style in the workplace. These people are respected among their colleagues and can share their ideas and thoughts openly and confidently with others. They have no problem taking on new challenges but are never afraid to say "no" or create strict boundaries.

Those individuals:

- Use frequent gestures
- Have great sharing abilities and collaboration skills
- Have a good posture
- Speak in a clear voice
- Are able to make friendly eye contact
- Express their thoughts and feelings effectively

When dealing with an assertive communicator, you should encourage them to speak up. If possible, give them leadership roles and ask them to help people with other communication styles. Work out what type of communicator you are from the information provided in this chapter. You can learn all about active listening in the following chapter. Active listening is among the most critical communication skills, which is why you'll benefit from learning how to improve on that front.

Chapter 2: How to Truly Listen

Do you ever feel like you're just sitting there, not contributing to a conversation you're listening to? You shouldn't feel uninvolved because communication requires both the speaker and the listener.

Communication requires both the speaker and the listener.
https://www.pexels.com/photo/photo-of-women-talking-to-each-other-4051134/

The speaker is the one who sends the message during communication, while the listener is the one who receives it. Communication breaks down if there is any break in the delivery by the speaker and the listener is confused or does not understand the message. There is a disconnect between the speaker and the listener.

This is about more than just hearing. It's also about comprehending what you hear, which tells you that the listener is just as important as the speaker. Effective listening is a necessary skill because it helps the listener understand and process the message being sent and, as a result, respond or act in the right way. This also helps the speaker.

So, we must learn how to truly listen. Does that sound strange? Even if it does, you should know that being silent during a conversation or a lecture does not really mean that you are paying attention.

You'll realize this when there's a small silence in the conversation, and you find yourself at a loss to describe what you've heard so far. If you're really listening, you'll instantly pick up on the main points of the message being conveyed and be able to rephrase it in your own words so that it keeps its authenticity and intention when it's conveyed to another listener.

If you can do this, it means you have listened to the message in its entirety without skimming, interrupting, or otherwise disrupting the speaker, and you understand what was being said.

If you want to be a good communicator, you must first learn to truly listen. In other words, before being a good communicator, you must first be an effective listener.

This will be covered in depth in the sections below.

What Is Effective Listening?

When you listen effectively, you pay attention to what is said, process the information correctly, and respond appropriately. As you can see, it goes beyond simply listening. Effective listening skills help boost your awareness, as well as your communication habits.

Importance of Effective Listening

As you learn to be a more effective listener, you'll find that your productivity and output grow. You'll be more in tune with the discussion and ready to tackle the challenge at hand. You can get the job done without making any mistakes or having to start again.

Listening also plays a large part in relationships. When people make concerted efforts to listen to one another, they develop better attitudes toward each other. This builds trust and a healthier relationship.

The following are the benefits of effective listening in everyday settings.

Effective Listening in Management and Supervision

The ability to listen attentively is crucial for any manager, whether they deal with human resources or oversee projects.

This ability helps you understand what your coworkers are saying at work, make sense of what is being said by those working with you on some projects, progress, process the information you have received, and make sound decisions based on it.

Managing people can be challenging because each person has their own quirks and communication styles. Dealing with this puts a lot of pressure on you, which could impact your attention to detail due to stress. However, if you have developed excellent and effective listening skills in the course of your life and studies, you will be able to play your part in the communication chain and deliver messages clearly.

Benefits of Effective Listening in Parenting

Parenting necessitates good listening skills for a variety of reasons. It's common knowledge that kids are never-ending chatterboxes because they constantly try to get their thoughts across and have no filters.

But within that stream of consciousness will be vital information you must not miss - don't tune out and let it become background noise. You must pay close attention until you understand what they are attempting to communicate to you, and this will, in turn, help you understand what they are saying and respond appropriately.

A good parent pays close attention to their children, not just to what they say but also to what they do – by reading their behavior. Therefore, listening helps you understand your children even beyond what they say.

The following are some of the ways that effective listening can improve your relationship with your children, which apply to both genders and ages:

1. Strengthening Your Relationship

Listening effectively to your children builds trust between you. They gain confidence in you because you can understand what upsets them. It also makes them easily confide in you. This strengthens your relationship and communication with them.

2. Conflict Resolution

Conflict resolution can be simple if you pay close attention to conversations. Listening effectively will help you understand differences from the children's perspectives, so you'll be able to react in a way that indicates you understand what's going on – and why – allowing you to address them appropriately.

Your children want to know that what they have previously said to you registered in your mind. You don't want to keep asking the same questions repeatedly because it will escalate the conflict.

If you listen to your kids closely enough, or anyone else in similar situations, for that matter, you can avoid arguments and build a better relationship with them.

3. Respect and Commitment

Effective listening demonstrates your love and concern for your children. Making them feel heard shows them you care, which builds commitment and respect in your relationship with them.

Effective Listening in Mentorship

If you are chosen to be someone's mentor, your listening skills will have to be sharpened. This is a position of responsibility and needs dedication. You need to make sure you listen carefully to your mentee, so good listening skills to be a good mentor. How essential is effective listening in mentoring? Let's cover that below.

3. Identifying Issues and Coming up with Solutions

Good listening skills will assist you in recognizing issues raised by your mentee, even if they have only expressed them nonverbally. You'll be able to decode those unspoken words, allowing you to search for and provide a solution. This is only possible if you pay close attention during conversations.

If you don't, you'll misunderstand your mentee, which could cause problems in your relationship because you won't be able to help solve problems or teach them what they need if you don't know their problems.

4. Building Trust between Both Mentor and Mentee

The relationship between a mentor and a mentee depends on many things, but trust is crucial. Mentees are more likely to be honest about their lives and struggles if they have confidence in you.

This trust, though, can't be built unless you have good listening skills, which will help them talk to you as they get to know you better over time.

5. Avoiding Conflicts Due to Communication Gaps

Conflicts are to be expected in all relationships, including those between mentors and mentees.

There may be times when you and your mentee have opposing viewpoints on specific issues. However, as the mentor, you have a responsibility to keep an open mind to their points of view and perspectives.

You will never understand their points of view if you are not a good listener.

You can encourage your mentee to share their thoughts and feelings by listening attentively and then asking leading questions. When you put yourself in their shoes, you gain a better understanding of their perspective and can use that to pave the way for more open lines of communication.

Listening Fosters Stronger Romantic Bonds

Listening is something that relationship specialists and therapists always emphasize. Unfortunately, many relationship problems can be traced back to a breakdown in any kind of communication in the relationship.

When people take the time to listen to each other, they create an environment where everyone feels comfortable sharing their thoughts and feelings without fear of criticism. Many troubled marriages experience this trouble because the partners have got into the habit of constantly cutting each other off and talking over one another, so this may take some time to change.

A trained couple's therapist may organize listening activities between couples to help with the process.

Listening Strengthens Friendships

Listening not only strengthens romantic and professional bonds but also strengthens friendships. If you're having trouble mending fences with longtime friends or connecting with new people, practicing active listening skills may be the answer.

Listening strengthens friendships by increasing trust, reducing misunderstandings, and increasing empathy. You should make an effort because it pays off.

Benefits of Effective Listening in Sales and Marketing

To be a successful salesman or marketer, good communication skills are a prerequisite, and your communication skills are not complete if you are not an effective listener.

One of your goals in communicating with potential customers and clients should be to gain insight into their needs and concerns concerning what you are selling and your products and services, as well as finding out information about your competitors' offerings and how you can use this information to improve your own offerings and attract more customers.

You won't be able to answer a question if you haven't read the situation in depth or listened adequately to your prospect's questions. Listening effectively to your prospective customers or clients has the following advantages:

- Your prospect will have faith in you because you have demonstrated that you value them by listening to them
- If the prospect discovers that you are more interested in meeting their needs than in making sales, they will be more willing to offer additional solutions and make necessary recommendations to you
- They will also be less reserved with you because you have shown your willingness to listen to them
- They believe in you and the solution that your products or services provided
- You can concentrate your efforts on those who genuinely require the product you provide

Remember that you are here to satisfy your customers as much as you are here to make sales. Therefore, listening effectively will reassure your customer that you care more about their satisfaction than your sales. This demonstrates to the customer that you genuinely care about their success, not just your own.

Show that you value every one of your customers. Give each of them the attention they need and make sure you personally attend to their needs and don't pass them off to someone else, as that is the quickest way to lose customers.

When you listen to each customer well enough, you'll make them feel that they are your top priority, which earns you their trust and commitment. Make no pretense about it. In all honesty, pay attention because if you don't, your client will find out, and you'll miss out on some information that may be crucial to your success in the long run.

Sometimes you already have a solution to a customer's problem. It is not a good idea to deny them the opportunity to express themselves because they will feel unimportant, and talk over them with your solution. Give them respect by giving them time to speak, and when they've finished, give them your response, but this time, modify it to fit what they've just described to you but echo some of the words they have used in their explanation.

Your effective listening skills will help you solve the same problem with different customers in different ways.

Effective listening will get you to reach an agreement quickly and unambiguously, providing solutions your customer is more likely to accept. If you can't listen, your sales rate will decrease, hurting your overall effectiveness – *and your pocket.*

Techniques for Effective Listening

1. Smiling

Smiling while listening to your speaker can help you listen more effectively. It assures the person speaking to you that they have your undivided attention and keeps you connected to them while they talk.

2. Leaning Forward

This is yet another effective listening technique. While someone is speaking to you, you adjust your posture to lean forward rather than sink back into your chair. When you lean forward, it's easier to block out background noise and concentrate on the speaker. It also gives them the impression that they have your full attention.

3. Eye Contact

Maintaining eye contact with the speaker while he is speaking is essential. This allows you to connect beyond the words they're saying. You can follow their gestures, facial expressions, and body language while they speak.

4. Paraphrasing the Speaker's Words

By attempting to paraphrase the speaker's words, you are already making sense of what they are saying, which dramatically improves your listening skills, as well as reassuring the person speaking to you that they have been heard.

5. Showing Concern

You can't show concern for the speaker if you don't follow up on the conversation. So, showing concern is beneficial to both you and the speaker. As you try to incorporate yourself into their narratives, it creates a bond and a sense of understanding between the two of you.

6. Asking for Clarification

Asking for clarification on ambiguous points is a great way to show that you're paying attention during a conversation or a chat. When something is not clear, be quick to ask for clarification, which, when provided, helps you understand what is being discussed better.

7. Summarizing

Your ability to summarize what has been said and pick the necessary points in the conversation is all part of effective listening. It helps you understand the message better and lets you build on it in your own way while keeping the main points in mind.

8. Acknowledging Verbally

During a conversation, verbal acknowledgment is vital to show that you are an effective listener. Verbal acknowledgment allows you to flow with the speaker as if you already know what he will say next. You're participating in the conversation and aren't missing anything, so you add a word to confirm something every now and then.

9. Highlighting Your Own Experiences

Finally, highlighting your own experience is on the list of techniques to improve effective listening. You can identify various points where the speaker said things that resonate with you as they speak.

How to Improve Your Listening Skills

Stick to a regular routine of reflection and contemplation. This will help you clear your mind and improve your concentration over time, which will reflect on your listening and communication methods.

Learn about the different types of listening and practice them regularly. Different types of listening include active listening, passive listening, critical listening, expansive listening, and reductive listening.

When you are in a noisy environment, try to listen to the different types of noise, figure them out one at a time, and isolate them. By doing so, you will acquire the ability to selectively tune out irrelevant sounds and maintain focus on the things you want to hear.

Find educational audio and video content and listen to it. This will significantly improve your listening skills while providing additional benefits such as education, motivation, etc. Check out things on YouTube, TV and radio shows, podcasts, etc.

You can do it while waiting for a train, driving, riding on the bus, or in any other spare moment.

Effective listening is a skill that will benefit you in many areas of your life. Developing this skill will have a hugely positive impact on your interpersonal relationships, and there are many lessons to be learned along the way. For example, you'll find out that you can't be an effective listener if you are doing all the talking. This teaches you to be quiet while listening, among other things.

When you let others speak before you respond, you can learn as much as possible about the topic and provide helpful feedback.

Keep an open mind when listening to pick out the critical details among the sea of spoken words. Don't let yourself get distracted too often, as it's possible that crucial information is being communicated just when you're about to lose focus.

Distractions can come in many forms, including off-topic conversations, interruptions from friends, and even cell phone ringing.

Keep your attention on the gestures and words, and jot down ideas as they come to you; you never know which one will come in handy.

Knowing that the message is more important than the messenger at that moment will help you improve. You could miss out on plenty of relevant details if you try to force the two together. Opportunity knocks when we realize that great ideas can come from people who may not share our values or beliefs.

Listening to responses or giving a counter-opinion is different from *listening to understand.* With the first type of listening, your mind is closed, only looking for the next opportunity to talk. But with the second, you have an open mind, you want to learn, and you want to learn essential things from what you hear.

In general, maintain your curiosity. Never close your mind to any issue; always be open to opposing viewpoints.

Knowing that your opinion on a subject may not be final will cause you to always ask questions that will enlighten you. It is not polite to interrupt people mid-sentence. It shows a lack of respect for the speaker and is very discouraging, and you risk losing sight of what is most important.

Be patient with those who may not be eloquent or quick with their words. Some people take longer than others to convey the same message. You should be aware of which applies to your speakers and give them the same value as anyone else.

Consistently demonstrate empathy and connection with your speaker. Demonstrate in your listening that you've processed the speaker's message and can relate to it. However, while showing empathy and connection, it is essential to maintain complete emotional control. Regardless of the speaker's attempts to push or pressure you with their words, you must maintain emotional control.

Always pay attention to body language while listening. Many things are communicated without words during a conversation, and you will miss them if you are not attentive enough.

If you put your mind to it, nothing is impossible to learn. In the same way, honing your existing skillset or learning new skills can have a significant impact.

Chapter 3: 5 Ways to Hear the Emotions behind the Words

Soft skills, such as effective communication, are highly valued in today's world and help improve cooperation and productivity in communities, workplaces, and at home. Global and local events have a way of distorting people's emotions and, in most cases, impair their ability to express themselves effectively. People frequently hide their true feelings behind a wall of words, making communication difficult.

Effective communication is more than just sharing information.
https://www.pexels.com/photo/pensive-ethnic-man-listening-to-answer-in-paper-cup-phone-3760607/

Words are an important part of our communication as humans, and expressing yourself, especially if you're in a vulnerable state, can be difficult. Notwithstanding, for effective communication to occur, any conversation must be founded on the pillars of empathy, emotional intelligence, and emotional awareness. To communicate, all parties must be able to understand themselves and others.

The speaker should be able to communicate their deepest feelings, and the listener should use logic to comprehend the message. Suppose the speaker appears to be hiding their emotions. In that case, the listener should be able to persuade the other party to communicate effectively by using emotional intelligence and emotional awareness.

Effective communication is more than just sharing information. The emotions behind the message must also be understood. Many things and so much outside noise can obstruct effective communication. The best results require a lot of effort.

This chapter examines how empathy, emotional awareness, and emotional intelligence affect the context of communication and how to understand people's expressions better.

Empathy, Emotional Awareness, Emotional Intelligence and Their Importance in Communication

Empathy is the ability to emotionally comprehend the feelings of others by viewing things from their point of view and imagining yourself in their situation. It means being aware of, sensitive to, and experiencing other people's thoughts and feelings. One can imagine themselves in the person's shoes and feel their emotions.

Emphatic people are good listeners, can recognize the feelings of others, are very helpful to people who find themselves in complex social situations, and provide excellent advice and assistance to those in need.

Empathy may be affective, somatic, or cognitive. Affective empathy is the ability to understand and respond appropriately to another person's feelings and emotions, whereas somatic empathy is the ability to have physical reactions in response to what another person is feeling. **Cognitive reaction** *is understanding and predicting another person's response to a situation.*

Empathy is instrumental in the context of communication. It enables you to communicate effectively with others because you understand and identify with them and can express yourself appropriately. Empathy facilitates forming of strong social bonds, which begin with meaningful conversations. It helps you moderate your emotions, which is beneficial in discussions because you'll then be able to communicate smoothly, even under different circumstances, such as when you're happy, stressed, or depressed, without pushing others away or imposing your opinions on them.

Emotional awareness is often confused with emotional intelligence; it comprises the ability to understand and recognize your own emotions and the emotions of others. It includes comprehending emotions and separating them, which aids communication.

People who are emotionally aware are good communicators because they understand their emotions and use them effectively to influence their conversations and ensure the message they want is communicated. They are aware of other people's emotions and communicate in a way that is reciprocal to those emotions.

Emotions are essential in communication, and awareness of them allows for effective communication. You will quickly learn to put measures in place to have progressive conversations. Most emotional responses can be predicted, and you can make better decisions because you know what actions are triggered by such emotions.

You will easily navigate and communicate your emotional phase, making communication easier and more fulfilling. Understanding one another is the heart of communication, and being aware allows you to do just that. It brings more joy and fulfillment. Thus incorporating this quality into a relationship or conversation makes communication more meaningful and memorable.

People with high emotional awareness have flourishing relationships because communication is always fluid and interesting. They can connect because they can converse openly and smoothly. They have done the work with themselves, which leads to a deep understanding of emotions - both theirs and their partner's, and if the relationship hits a rough patch, emotions can be confronted head-on so that the balance in the relationship is restored.

Emotional intelligence, like emotional awareness, refers to the ability to comprehend, apply, perceive, handle, and manage emotions. It is defined as a set of traits and skills that influence performance and leadership. It is the interface between your emotional and cognitive functions. And it's at this meeting point you can deduce people's emotions and respond appropriately.

It includes self-management, social awareness, and relationship management. Controlling impulsive behaviors, managing your emotions, knowing your limits, recognizing the feelings of others, understanding your own and their impact on others, being socially comfortable, inspiring great relationships, and clearly communicating with colleagues, friends, and those around you are all part of it.

It is a social skill that can be learned or inherited. It entails evaluating, recognizing, and controlling your own emotions and the emotions of others, using emotional information to guide behavior and thinking, discern and label different feelings, and shape them for adaptation to the environment.

People with high emotional intelligence are self-assured, curious, emphatic, sensitive, and concerned about others. They're reliable, admit mistakes and accept change. Emotionally intelligent people can communicate with sensitivity and understanding in their workplace and personal lives. Conflicts are unavoidable during conversations with people, and with emotional intelligence, you can effectively communicate in a way that resolves the conflict.

Understanding emotions help you to develop fruitful relationships with colleagues and acquaintances. Emotions influence communication, and understanding your feelings is integral to effective communication. Self-control is the ability to read situations and respond appropriately, and expressing yourself without aggression in stressful or uncomfortable situations are all emotional intelligence traits.

Emotional intelligence can improve teamwork and relationships in the workplace or family. It helps you discuss and reach compromises with opposing factions on various topics, generating togetherness. Evaluating your own and other people's emotions allows you to avoid conflicts, stay relaxed, and create a happy work team.

Being emotionally intelligent also lets you encourage and motivate people during difficult times; it gives you self-confidence, which allows you to approach people, assess situations, and provide helpful information to help them overcome their feelings. To achieve effective verbal and nonverbal communication, you must pay attention to emotions and words.

Communication involves more emotion than information.

Empathy, emotional intelligence, and awareness are all skills that can help you communicate more effectively. They improve your ability to feel, control, use, and comprehend not only your own emotions but also the emotions of others. This is a valuable asset in families and workplaces, and developing these skills is critical in the context of communication.

5 Ways to Better Understand People's Expressions

Understanding people's expressions or the message they're conveying is essential to have productive conversations. Empathy allows you to put yourself in the shoes of others and see things from their perspective, while emotional awareness will enable you to read the situation, express yourself appropriately, and make tangible connections.

Using these skills individually or together facilitates emotional information and development. It enhances your ability to read meaning into the expressions and messages of others while attempting to persuade and lift their spirit. It takes a lot of effort to try to understand people. However, empathy, emotional intelligence, and emotional awareness can help.

Here are some strategies to help you understand what people may be trying to express:

1. Improved Self-Control with Emotional Intelligence

Being calm and in control of your emotions improves communication and allows you to see things from the perspective of others. Your feelings influence your communication, and controlling them will enable you to interact with others more effectively.

Emotional intelligence lets you control your thoughts, feelings, and utterances when under stress and helps you respond reflectively. It improves your self-control, prevents your emotions and nerves from getting the better of you, and instead of speaking quickly or aggressively, you remain calm and can hold reasonable conversations.

Understanding people's expressions at work requires emotional intelligence. Stress, workload, and pressure are common in the workplace. Responding inappropriately or misinterpreting a piece of information can lead to arguments, conflicts, or even work being undone. However, by exercising emotional intelligence, you can gain control of the situation, understand the feelings of others, and respond constructively. Understanding others makes you approachable and lets you influence their emotions. If you understand people, you can prevent or minimize conflicts, work through frustration, and foster happiness in the home or office. You get to cheer them up, talk through their emotions, and build better working relationships, which ultimately increases productivity.

2. Reading Situations

Emotional intelligence is the ability to decipher not only your own feelings but also those of others. Understanding other people's emotions and making sense of the environment around you makes it easier to reach compromises and productive solutions using effective and meaningful communication.

This implies self-regulation, listening, and responding in a conversation. You understand how to keep your responses convenient, subdue impulsive reactions, and slow down before expressing strong or critical opinions.

Reacting on impulse to the expressions of others creates a communication gap, which is unhealthy, while understanding how the other party feels, gaining insight into their mental or emotional state, attempting to put yourself in their shoes, or experiencing what they're going through allows you to make rational decisions. When you combine emotional intelligence and emotional awareness, you can better understand people.

When having a conversation with a friend who is experiencing anxiety, heartbreak, or loss, emotional intelligence advises you on the best course of action to take and reminds you to actively listen rather than bugging the person with your own concerns. You will be able to tell if the time is right to express your deepest feelings, a new idea, or a discovery during such conversations. You will know when and how to respond.

When a friend needs someone to listen to them, it's going to be emotional intelligence that will help you to determine whether you should speak or just listen. It enables you to assess the situation, adapt to it, and provide an appropriate solution to the conversation. You will understand when to participate and when to remain silent during a conversation. You will avoid conflict, prevent issues from exacerbating, and be diplomatic in your dealings with others.

3. **Empathy and Understanding**

Empathy entails relating to and comprehending the emotions of others. Viewing things from the perspective of others and attempting to experience how they feel improves communication and relationships in homes, offices, and colleges. Empathy is essential in communication. It entails comprehending the circumstances of others and the feelings that the situation may elicit in the individual. After identifying what a person is attempting to express or what they are experiencing, the next step is to try to relate to that situation.

Cultivate empathy, as it's crucial to understand what is happening with other people and think like them. To be effective at helping others, you need to observe their words and actions. If you work at the same place, look at their working conditions or attitude to work, ask emphatic questions to find out what's causing the trouble, try to understand how they feel, and get them to talk more about the situation.

If your boss or a colleague exhibits irritable behavior at work, don't react similarly. Instead, figure out what's wrong, try to understand how they're feeling, and offer assistance as needed and appropriate. To understand people, you must put yourself in their shoes and see things from their perspective. This allows you to assist them and interact more suitably. With empathy, you can avoid conflicts and set realistic expectations for yourself and your relationship with your boss, colleague, or friend.

4. **Reflection before Reaction**

Emotions influence how you perceive, understand, handle, and respond to others. Understanding other people's emotions requires us to empathize before taking action or offering a solution relevant to that situation. Combining empathy, emotional intelligence, and emotional awareness allows you to read, relate, and respond to a situation appropriately and on time.

Human emotions are a tangled web for anyone to navigate, but getting to the point between mental and emotional functionality allows you to see what's going on before taking action. To fully understand what others are feeling, you must first master your own emotions. Taking control of your own emotions prevents you from being aggressive, demanding, or unhelpful to the person you are talking to, and understanding the emotions of others makes it easier to help them.

You will be able to detect and collect emotional and mental data, examine and interpret it, and then be helpful with a proper response. You will be able to think about what is in front of you and respond appropriately. You'll know when it's appropriate to respond or remain passive while listening and offering assistance as needed.

5. Build Trust

Effective communication cannot occur without trust. Building trust with the individual lays the groundwork for a good conversation. Looking at things through their eyes and getting them to open up can only happen if there is trust. You never know how far something as simple as a handshake can go. Making eye contact, and sitting beside or in front of the person, can help you to start a conversation.

Since you can put yourself in their shoes and emotional intelligence allows you to predict the emotions which may lead to a specific action, talk to them as if you are in the same situation. If you've been there, describe your experience and how you overcame it. Trust is essential to understand others, so be careful not to lose it as you build your social and work circles.

Recognizing flaws and mistakes can occur when understanding people keeps the conversation moving. Helping the person understand that mistakes do happen can also assist them in admitting their feelings, opening up, and having those difficult conversations.

Misunderstandings occur at work, at home, and even with friends, but they can be avoided if you use your emotional intelligence. A colleague may be angry over past events, or a child or teacher may have annoyed a family member, who then acted out against you. With emotional intelligence, you can reflect on your response and agree that a past event or circumstance may have caused that behavior while fully understanding that you have done nothing wrong to warrant that degree of reaction. Understanding emotions greatly helps effective communication. Demonstrating care, empathy, and intelligence when dealing with emotional conversations and situations also helps communication.

How to Improve Relationally and Evaluate the Emotions of Others

Developing emotionally and attempting to deduce the emotions others hide behind their words is a difficult task. Emotional skills are extremely beneficial, and while they can be innate, they can also be learned. With consistent practice and dedication, you can substantively read meaning into the messages and expressions of others.

Exercises for emotional development and emotion deduction include:

Practicing Mindfulness

Your mind is a vast space that houses your thoughts, feelings, and emotions. Thus, learning how to comprehend and focus on a specific event will help you understand others. It will be easier to relate to others if you can train your mind to focus on the present moment, pay attention to a conversation, and not make snap judgments.

Mindfulness is how you appreciate different moments in life and experience physical and mental sensations. It allows you to remain calm, see things from a different perspective, and stay focused. You'll be able to control your emotions and those of others by practicing mindfulness.

Prioritize Listening

Active listening is the most effective way to read emotional messages from people. Keep your mind open and present in the conversation while actively listening to what the other person has to say. You can't help someone if you don't know what's wrong, and you can't know what's wrong if you don't listen. When a friend calls to express their dismay or frustration, you can't hear the emotions behind the words spoken if you're distracted.

You can also put yourself in their shoes if they contact you via text, and you should try to read their intent. Look for verbal cues such as voice tones or nonverbal cues during conversations. If they insist they're fine and have things under control, take their word for it but follow up with subsequent conversations.

Explore Differences

You can't give good advice if you have a rigid mindset and lifestyle. You'll tell them to be like you rather than assisting them by seeing beyond their emotions. Investigate other cultures, solicit other people's opinions, try out new things and always be curious.

Try to see or experience things from their perspective. You don't want to help someone and then be told, "You don't know what it's like." You may not have grown up or experienced things the same way they did, but having an idea, insight, or inkling of what it's like to be them can help you understand others.

Offer Help

Putting yourself in the person's shoes or feeling their pain isn't enough on its own. Try to lift them up as well. Feelings are nice, but they aren't enough. What matters is what you do. Take the risk if you can provide physical assistance to alleviate the pain, stress, or discomfort.

To lighten the mood and reduce the burden, use humor and laughter, which are natural stress antidotes. Empathy and emotional awareness are useful, but if you can offer assistance, the person will likely appreciate it more.

Communication is more about emotions than information, so understanding emotions is essential to effective communication. It is difficult to discuss emotions and how they affect our everyday communication, and understanding how our moods, feelings, and states of mind can be expressed or concealed behind words or other forms of expression can improve or degrade communication.

Empathy, emotional awareness, and emotional intelligence all play important roles in communication. Using them can help you understand the emotions expressed in other people's words. You must be able to handle, manage, and perceive your own emotions and the emotions of others, all while using emotional awareness and emotional intelligence to control your thoughts and potential responses to a situation.

Emotional development aims to achieve this by paying attention not only to words but also to the genuine message conveyed within statements made. Being emotionally sound, aware, and responsible to others facilitates better relationships and conversations.

Paying attention, actively listening, and being mindful of your response are all strategies to employ. It is not enough to feel and experience the pain of others. You must also build trust and, when necessary, take action. Only then can you fully realize the potential of effective communication.

Chapter 4: How Body Language Can Make or Break a Conversation

We have been told time and time again to "Think before we speak," but merely following this golden principle is highly unlikely to lead to fruitful conversations. Words constitute only around 30% of the message conveyed in a conversation, and 70% of what is absorbed by the listener depends on your body language and tone of voice. So, choosing the right words is only a small part of the equation.

Body language includes all the non-verbal cues.
https://www.pexels.com/photo/woman-with-steepled-fingers-7320508/

Body language is the silent form of communication that plays a vital role in a conversation. It includes all the non-verbal cues, gestures, posture, facial expressions, and tone as well. Body language conveys more than words.

Impact of Body Language

It is a little alarming that body language plays such a huge part in communication, yet we are mostly unaware of what our body is doing while speaking. Bad body language is off-putting, offensive, and sometimes hurtful. It is also necessary to actively learn to understand and practice positive non-verbal cues to have more pleasant conversations.

Body language helps us to understand others and express ourselves in a better way. You can understand the emotions and thoughts in a person's head through body language. For instance, a tilted head and direct eye contact can show that the person is interested in the conversation and listening carefully.

Body language can help you understand people better and build strong relationships with them. It can also help you interpret someone's reaction to something you're saying. For instance, if someone frowns at you, it means that they are angry or don't agree with your opinions. Your body language can be intentional or unintentional, positive or negative. Once you learn more about it, you can eliminate unintentional negative traits and intentionally incorporate positive ones. Learning about body language can help you communicate effectively and make you more confident and appealing.

How Body Language Can Be a Communication Barrier

Body language can become a communication barrier because it speaks more than words do. For instance, if someone is talking about a sensitive matter, and you say, "I'm listening," but you don't exhibit any facial expressions to back up your words, chances are there that they won't believe you and may stop talking to you. Suppose it's apparent from your body language that you're nervous or anxious. In that case, people may find this off-putting enough to avoid talking to you. A person who avoids eye contact, keeps their head down, and has a slouchy posture will be considered disinterested in the conversation. However, positive body language attracts people to start communicating with you and to continue to communicate.

Types of Non-Verbal Communication

1. **Facial expressions** are the first thing that a person will see while talking to you. If your expressions make you seem disinterested, there's no way that your words will assure the other person that you're really interested.
2. **Gestures** - Waving your hand to say hello is a kind gesture. You can also use gestures to support your words, such as a thumbs up when you agree to something.
3. **Eye contact** -Making eye contact can emphasize your presence. Rolling your eyes is a sign of displeasure or irritation. The eyes are a window to one's soul and can express a lot.
4. **Posture** - Your posture can indicate your comfort level, self-esteem, confidence, and interest in the conversation.
5. **Proxemics** -The use of distance while communicating.
6. **Paralanguage** -This includes how you talk, tone, speaking speed, pitch, and loudness.
7. **Haptics** -This refers to the body language which involves touch, such as hugging, handshakes, and holding hands.

How to Interpret Emotions from One's Body Language

You can read a person's body language from the different parts of the body, including their eyes, hands, face, and feet. Observing all these and coming to a conclusion is better than interpreting something by looking at a single part. Sometimes a person may not be able to express what he wants to, but his body language will get his message across.

For instance, if your friend is telling you that he's fine, but his eyes are watery, his tone is shaky, and he's not smiling, then you may conclude that he's upset about something but isn't comfortable sharing it. You can encourage him to share his problems with you and make him realize that you won't judge him; you'll simply listen to him with empathy, which may help him open up to you and build a better bond.

Facial expressions alone can show so much about what a person is feeling, and that's why they're considered a universal form of communication. Eminent American researcher and psychologist Paul

Ekman has published plenty of papers on the subject to confirm how important facial expressions are to communication.

Even if there was no language, you would still be able to understand other person's emotions through their facial expressions. A smiling face shows happiness, while frowning is a sign of sadness. Anger, fear, confusion, excitement, and desire are all emotions that can be understood just by observing facial expressions.

Other body parts also play a vital role in understanding emotion. Think about a person sitting beside you, constantly biting his nails and shaking his legs. You would be able to understand that he's either stressed or anxious. There wasn't a single exchange of words between you, but you understood his state of mind by observing his body language. That shows the importance of body language in understanding feelings, emotions, and moods.

Positive Non-Verbal Cues

Often, we're unaware of our non-verbal communication through our body movements, gestures, and posture. By knowing more about positive non-verbal cues, you can incorporate these consciously into your daily life. It will help you communicate better and leave a remarkable first impression of your personality with those who meet you.

These are some of the most important examples of positive non-verbal cues.

1. Good Posture

A good posture conveys that you are not nervous, anxious, or confused. To maintain good posture, be mindful of your head, shoulders, and back position. Keeping your head high, shoulders relaxed, and back straight will make you look comfortable and confident.

2. Leaning In

It is important to keep your back straight when you are talking because it shows confidence. However, when the other person is talking, leaning in a little is a proven way of showing interest and empathy. You can make the speaker more comfortable by leaning in because this sends out a message that you are totally invested in the conversation.

3. Eye Contact

This is not an easy one. Too little or too much of it can ruin the entire conversation. Breaking eye contact every now and then so that it doesn't look like you are staring is part of effective communication and conversation.

4. Arms

Crossing your arms in front of you is like holding up a shield to defend yourself from attack. This gesture indicates that you could be scared and defensive and are ready to finish the conversation as soon as possible. If this is not the message you wish to convey, hang your arms comfortably by your side. If you are sitting, bringing your hands together in your lap is a good way to show interest and eagerness.

How to Appear Confident

A straight posture is an essential positive non-verbal cue that can help you appear confident. If you slouch and cross your arms or legs, try to get out of this habit, as it indicates social anxiety and makes you appear less confident. Don't put your hands in your pockets and look down while speaking/walking because those gestures also make you appear anxious and nervous. If you have a habit of moving your legs, biting your nails, or shaking your knees, try to control them. It won't be easy at first, but it'll enhance your personality and make you appear more confident.

Always make eye contact while listening or speaking because it shows that you're paying attention and are interested in the conversation. Making eye contact while speaking is a sign that you feel confident and positive about the subject you are discussing.

Always shake hands firmly - not too tight and not too open. This may be simple, but it can reveal a lot about your personality. Slow down your movements when you move forward to shake hands, as fast and vigorous movements can be interpreted as anxiety.

The appropriate tone of voice is a crucial positive non-verbal cue. It's not what you say, but it is how you speak. You can lift your communication skills by working on your tone, pitch, and pauses between your words.

Positive nonverbal cues show you're interested in the conversation.

Head Nodding

If you nod your head whenever you agree with another person's point of view, it'll show that you're paying attention. Nodding your head with a smile indicates that you're interested and enthusiastic about the conversation.

Open Palms

Open palms say that you're not defensive but are open to whatever the other person is saying. It means you're receiving their opinion and ideas openly without any defensiveness.

Leaning Forward

Leaning forward in a conversation is interpreted as a sign of engagement and interest in the conversation. It shows that you want to hear the speaker better.

Making Eye Contact

Eye contact can make the speaker feel that they're being heard. Although making eye contact is really important, don't do it to the extent that it starts to make the other person feel uncomfortable.

Positive Non-Verbal Cues That Show Empathy

Relaxed Face

A relaxed face can show that you have a soft personality. Softness is the key to empathy. Keep stern looks for when you mean to be stern, and look gently at the other person. Smile more often to look more approachable.

Eyebrows

Your eyebrows can express a lot. While listening to someone, lifting your eyebrows can show that you're actually concerned about them. It shows that you're right there with them.

Voice

Your soft tone can do a lot more than you think. Speaking slowly and in a soft tone is a sign that you're gentle, calm, and caring.

Breathing

You may have noticed that your breathing changes during different emotions. When you're angry or frustrated, you'll find you breathe quicker. Try to breathe slowly, deeply, and calmly. It shows that you have a relaxed personality.

Use of Hands

You can use your hands while listening to others to show empathy. For instance, if someone is anxious, nervous, or stuck with a problem, you can hold and squeeze their hand to show that you want to be there for them. Putting a hand on someone's shoulder during a conversation also shows that you have a friendly personality.

Mirroring

Mirroring is basically copying/mimicking the other person's body language, tone, posture, etc. It shows that you're interested and totally engaged in the conversation. For instance, matching their tone, pace, and volume will show that you have the same energy and vibe. Mirroring is a form of active communication because when someone sees a reflection of himself in another person's actions, he automatically develops trust and gets comfortable being around them. Don't overdo it.

Negative Non-Verbal Cues

Negative non-verbal cues include gestures, postures, and expressions that may offend others or hurt and decrease your influence and respect. These can be intentional or unintentional. Negative non-verbal cues can affect your personal as well as professional life.

The following is a list of nonverbal cues that you need to avoid.

Maintaining Distance

Maintaining a certain healthy distance while communicating is really crucial. While communicating, it should never feel like you're invading the other person's personal space.

Check Your Facial Expressions

Sometimes we're unaware of the facial expressions we're giving to others. Negative facial expressions can really break up a conversation. Controlling your facial expressions is quite a tough job, but you can learn to do it by practicing in front of a mirror. You need to keep your face straight and relax. Loosen up your jaw and relax your forehead.

Constantly Touching Your Face and Hair

This may seem a harmless habit, but it shows that you're distracted and not interested in the conversation, hence finding ways to distract yourself. You may find this habit difficult to overcome, but being aware of it – and working on it gradually – will help you to stop it.

Covering Your Mouth

Covering your mouth during a conversation can show that you're either anxious or don't have confidence. Most people do that while being in group discussions, whether personal or professional office meetings.

Eye Contact

Avoiding eye contact can be interpreted as low confidence, lack of self-esteem, or fear due to lying. People don't look into someone else's eyes when they lie, so it could be misinterpreted if you have difficulty with this. However, it is considered disrespectful in some cultures, so you must judge depending on the situation.

Too much eye contact, i.e., staring, is also a negative non-verbal cue because it makes the other person uncomfortable.

Crossed Arms

This is known as a sign of either defensiveness or discomfort. It creates a barrier between you and the person you're communicating with. It either shows that you're uncomfortable or don't agree with their thoughts.

Hand Movements

Too many fast hand or body movements show you're anxious or nervous. Sweating while making a conversation is also a sign of anxiety.

Looking Away

Looking away at various objects (such as wall clocks and paintings) or constantly checking your phone can annoy the person you're communicating with. He may think that you're not interested in the conversation.

How Can Non-Verbal Communication Go Wrong?

How you communicate through your body language affects how people see you. You may add non-verbal cues unintentionally, but people don't ignore them. Sometimes you think you're doing everything right, but things go wrong because of those unintentional non-verbal cues. Below are some examples of how non-verbal communication can go wrong:

1. Jane is young, beautiful, and a smart woman. She has a good sense of humor and gets along with everyone. But still, she isn't able to build a long-term relationship or friendship because she constantly moves her legs, bites her nails, and has violent hand movements. She is constantly anxious, and anyone who's around her feels that too.

2. Simon is an empathetic person, he thinks he gets along with everyone in the office, but if you ask his co-workers, they don't

agree with that because they find him to be too intense. He doesn't maintain a healthy distance and invades everyone's private space. While shaking hands, he holds the other person's hand so firmly that it makes them feel uncomfortable.

3. Mike is a young boy who tries to be friendly but still doesn't have any friends. He can initiate friendships but can't make them last. This is because Mike's face turns red whenever someone gives his opinion, and his facial expressions show that he doesn't agree with them. This pushes everyone away from him.

4. Alexa congratulated Megan on her promotion, but Megan noticed the jealousy and sadness in her tone. So Megan could interpret that Alexa wasn't happy with her success.

Minor details that you do subconsciously play an important role in forming your image to those observing you.

How to Develop Better Non-Verbal Communication

Here are some tips that can be used in daily life to gradually develop your non-verbal communication skills:

Observe Yourself

You need to observe yourself and keep noticing all the unintentional non-verbal cues you use in your everyday life. Think about your normal posture and tone and how it changes during different emotions such as anger, sadness, and nervousness. Assess what needs to be changed and work on that.

Avoid Using Incompatible Non-Verbal Cues

Do you say that you're fine while moving your legs? This is a sign that you're giving mixed messages. The other person will understand that you're actually not fine but trying to hide your feelings.

Learn from Others

Observe what kind of non-verbal cues others use in order to express themselves or while making a conversation. For instance, if there's a confident person, you can watch him for cues that make him seem that way and try to copy them.

There's No Hard and Fast Rule

There's no strict rule that a certain non-verbal cue means a specific thing. The meaning of non-verbal cues can vary according to personal and cultural aspects. You need to ask before you assume. For instance, if someone is looking down while talking to you, you may ask him if he does that by habit or if something is upsetting him.

Relationship between Confidence and Body Language

Amy Cuddy is a Harvard University researcher who studied body language and its effect on confidence. According to her research, relaxed and open body language or high-power poses should boost confidence more than a closed and stiff body. High power poses increase testosterone and decreases cortisol, ultimately boosting confidence. Many people practice high-power poses in the morning to keep their confidence up throughout the day. Keeping your posture right the whole day will add up so much to your confidence levels.

Some common nonverbal interpretations:

- **Leaning towards a person:** This mostly shows that one is interested in the conversation but is sometimes interpreted as aggression.
- **Avoiding eye contact:** Can be interpreted as shyness, lack of confidence, no self-esteem, and even fear.
- **Crossing arms or legs:** Is mostly seen as defensiveness, but some people do it because they're nervous or because it is a habit.
- **Shaking/moving legs:** A sign of nervousness, anxiety, or boredom.
- **Forming a fist:** This shows aggression in most cases, but some people may do it because they feel threatened.
- **Eye roll:** Irritation, annoyance, or boredom.

Although understanding body language and learning how to interpret the common body language helps boost communication skills, there are no strict rules about these. It can vary according to the situation. For instance, putting a hand on someone's shoulder in the workplace could be considered a bad sign, but if you do that at a friend's meetup, it may be considered a friendly gesture. In the same way, this can also vary from person to person. Some people bite their nails because it's a habit and not due to anxiety or nervousness. If you're confused about someone's body language, you can always ask questions to help you to understand better. You can look at a person's body language as a whole instead of looking at individual signals to come to a better conclusion. For example, suppose someone is leaning forward, and you don't know whether he's doing that because he's interested or aggressive. In that case, you can observe the truth by looking at his facial expressions. If he's leaning forward while smiling, he's obviously interested in you and the conversation.

Good body language is not something you are born with or without. It is something you can learn, practice, and perfect. Having an important conversation without understanding and practicing positive non-verbal cues is like doing a plank without engaging your core. The former will hurt your muscles, and the latter will hurt your relationships.

Chapter 5: How to Spark up a Conversation...with Anyone

What better way to express yourself and help others understand you than through communication?

A great conversation can lead to both participants learning new things and give them wonderful memories to look back on in the future.
https://www.pexels.com/photo/photograph-of-men-having-conversation-seating-on-chair-1015568/

Even if you are an introvert, there are strategies you can employ to make any conversation easier. Striking up conversations with strangers can be very challenging, especially if you don't feel confident or have no interesting way to engage them.

All of your concerns and assumptions appear to be based solely on what is in your head. Starting a conversation is simple if you understand the person's personality well.

A great conversation can lead to both participants learning new things and give them wonderful memories to look back on in the future.

The key to success in social interactions like this is to develop some outstanding conversation starters that you can use to spark engaging conversations with anyone, whether in a business or social setting.

Watch the mood of the people around you and pick your moment to begin a conversation. By observing people, you can read the social cues and then be able to initiate a conversation. Choose your time carefully so you don't mess up your first impression on others.

How Communication Can Help You Build Social Relationships

Having good relationships with people lessens feelings of stress and anxiety. Your mental health will be in jeopardy, and your anxiety will increase if your relationships with others are unhealthy. This can cause you to avoid social situations and prevent you from developing positive relationships.

When you desperately want to make friends or meet new people but are afraid to make the first move, you can start to feel anxiety and mental stress.

The disadvantage of avoiding social relationships is that you will not be able to develop the confidence that comes from interacting with others. You won't be able to develop good communication skills that could have increased your chances of having successful relationships.

For example, suppose you are afraid of going on a date with someone, perhaps due to a lack of confidence or experience. In that case, you will be unable to handle situations such as knowing what to say or wear. You almost certainly have the ability but lack the confidence to put it to use. Below are some tips for starting a conversation.

Best Way to Initiate a Conversation

The first step toward developing a healthy social relationship is communicating your intentions and opinions, which do not have to be verbal. The vast majority of our interactions are non-verbal. Anyone who pays attention to your body language will generally pick up on your message.

A deaf person will get your message simply by watching your eye movements and other body language cues. You should be mindful of the signals your body sends out in social situations, as they could be interpreted in ways you didn't intend.

On the plus side, verbal and non-verbal communication skills can help you share knowledge, ideas, suggestions, and other valuable information with others, allowing you to form stronger bonds with them.

Communication is essential for social bonding; an easy way to start a conversation is by complimenting others. Make it about them or a random interesting topic instead of yourself. Allow others to speak and be a good listener because no one enjoys talking to someone who isn't attentive. If you show that you can accept and even appreciate different points of view, you'll encourage more conversation and gain the respect of your peers and anyone you interact with.

Communication makes you feel less anxious, improves your ability to talk to others, boosts your confidence, and lets you learn from others.

Strategies for Initiating Conversation with Strangers

Throughout your life, you will encounter different people in various settings. Knowing how to start a conversation with these new acquaintances can be difficult.

When you succeed in starting a conversation on a positive note, it can develop into something more interesting. Most of the time, we only have one chance to engage a stranger in conversation, and if we mess up that opportunity, everything else is ruined.

How you communicate with a stranger in an office differs from how you would communicate with someone in a grocery store.

Different scenarios dictate specific approaches. Starting a conversation with a stranger can be awkward, so you should know where and when to begin.

- Don't waste the stranger's time. Keep the conversation brief if you notice they are preoccupied.

Maintain your cool and confidence as you make the bold move of starting a conversation. Take a deep breath, and organize your thoughts. It won't look good if the stranger sees that you are nervous.

1. Keep a positive attitude and refrain from using body language that contradicts your intentions. Maintain eye contact and act friendly, as this will demonstrate that you are friendly and confident.
2. You can start with a question about something you have in common, such as the news, the weather, or their lunch choice - your situation will influence your subject. Consider questions or comments you can make about the subject as they respond to keep the conversation going.
3. Compliments work like magic when approaching strangers because most people enjoy being admired. You could say something like, "I really like your shoes." This complement may spark further conversation about the shoes. You must follow up with additional questions, such as whether other colors are available and where they purchased them. Not everyone will be willing to answer additional questions from you, but regardless of their response, keep a positive attitude.
4. Use something in your immediate surroundings to start a conversation. If you're in a restaurant, point to your favorite spot and invite the stranger to try it out.
5. You could also ask, "Do you live in this neighborhood? I saw your car pass mine the other day."
6. Do you want to keep things simple? Then you should start with an introduction. "Hello, my name is ... I recently moved into the neighborhood, and I come here every Friday to play tennis. I hope to see you around." This has given you some ideas for your next meeting. Remember that you're talking to a stranger, so don't tell them too much about yourself straight away to avoid boring them. Allow them to talk about themselves as well.
7. Help someone you don't know. Helping a stranger carry a box or bag is an ideal time to strike up a conversation. As you help them, ask them questions like, "Did you just move in here?" When you offer to help a stranger, and they say yes, use the opportunity to ask them other questions that don't involve you.
8. Be open to hearing other people's views. If you're out for lunch and can't decide which chicken dish to try, you can ask them

which one they prefer. Continue the conversation with related topics, and possibly ask to sit with them if they don't mind.

9. Keep up with current events and use a viral topic to start a conversation. As they respond, other interesting topics will emerge, and the conversation will flow.
10. Asking for assistance is also a good way to start a conversation. When you are new to a situation, ask for help with what you don't know or understand, and take advantage of the opportunity to start a great conversation.
11. When you meet people who share your interests, take advantage of the opportunity to discuss them, remembering to let them lead the conversation at first. This is a great way to get them excited about talking to you.
12. Make a remark that shows you have noticed the stranger. Say something like, "I noticed you write with your left hand. I am also left-handed." This will make the stranger feel more at ease and possibly open to further conversation.
13. When starting a conversation with a stranger, you can use your good sense of humor to make the stranger laugh. Tell jokes that aren't offensive and which are relevant to what's going on in your current location. Having a great sense of humor makes it easier to make friends and get along with others.

Tips for Making a Good First Impression

The importance of first impressions in forming social relationships cannot be overstated. What you communicate carries less weight than how you communicate.

Someone can form an opinion about you based on a single incidence of eye contact.

You may argue that judging people so quickly is unfair, and you may be right, but we're dealing with reality here, and assumptions are unavoidable. People who look at you will make many assumptions about you.

Some people cling to first impressions for far too long, despite everything. They believe their initial assessment is the most accurate and are adamant that they won't change their opinion. People having a negative first impression of you can ruin their potential relationship with you.

People use first impressions to filter characteristics in others that will be remembered in subsequent interactions. You'll hear things like, "I've always known you can't be trusted since the first time I laid eyes on you." It's difficult to change that first impression if it's not positive, so try to always make your first impression a positive and memorable one.

The persistence of first impressions can be attributed to our subconscious nature. Even when presented with contradicting evidence, our cognitive and implicit biases prevent us from revising our initial assessment.

You can think of first impressions as social capital that you can use to strengthen your bonds with others. Making a positive first impression can lead to new opportunities, especially if your experience and qualifications are a good fit.

Even if you are scared, act confidently to give the impression that you are confident. People will be drawn to you if you appear confident.

The following tips will help you to make a good first impression.

Appear Confident

When you are around people, your responsibility is to provide value; the only way to do so is to research and learn. Basic research on your surroundings will influence your decision on how to dress and whether bad language is acceptable. Preparing ahead of time will make you feel more at ease and show your focus and interest.

Give Emotional Support

Paying attention to the other person's emotions demonstrates your empathy. Emotional support will not only help you make a good first impression, but it will also help you form a strong connection with the other person. It shows that you care, and they will believe you are a loving person.

Good Body Language

Maintain positive body language because people can misinterpret it if you are slightly off. Deaf people rely heavily on non-verbal cues like facial expressions and gestures to make meaning of a conversation. Sit up straight and hold your head up to show confidence and comfort. Cross your legs and place your arms on your lap. As a welcoming gesture, offer a firm, though non-harmful, handshake.

Talk Less and Listen More

Be an excellent communicator who listens more and speaks less. To keep this going, make sure you talk less than half as much as you listen. Listening more demonstrates that you are attentive and love hearing about the other party. Making others feel good by listening well and communicating clearly is important.

Be Real

You are the best version of yourself, so stay true to yourself. It is easy to identify a fake, and you certainly wouldn't want that associated with your reputation. Simply be yourself and avoid attempting to prove a point during the first impression because this will come across as being insecure. Know your own weaknesses and strengths, and communicate them with care.

Dress Well

Isn't it true that the way you dress determines how you'll be addressed? People will make many assumptions about you based on what you wear. Whether you believe it or not, there are consequences for what you wear. For example, if you go to a job interview and dress casually, it will be assumed that you will not take the job seriously.

Smile Genuinely

A great first impression begins with a smile. People feel welcome and at ease around you when you wear a genuine smile. Don't force it because eyes don't lie. When you smile genuinely, it shows in your eyes and gives the impression that you are sincere and trustworthy.

Maintain Eye Contact

Eye contact is a nonverbal communication technique that shows respect for the person you are speaking with. Maintaining eye contact demonstrates that you are paying attention. Look the other person in the eyes before starting the conversation, and continue to do so throughout the conversation. Do not confuse staring at someone with correct eye contact.

Be Suggestive

If it's an official meeting, research the person and company to get a sense of what they're all about. Making informed contributions during a conversation will go a long way in demonstrating your commitment. Don't give your opinion too quickly. Instead, be suggestive so you don't make things worse or send the wrong message.

Bring a notebook to jot down notes if it's a business meeting. You don't want to be perceived as disengaged, so write something down even if you can remember it without writing it down.

Use Light Humor

A good sense of humor will help you to network with people in a less tense manner. Making them laugh or smile before you market your product is an excellent way to make a good first impression. Sarcasm should be avoided because it can backfire. Remember, you're talking to a stranger and have no idea how sensitive they are, so keep the jokes light.

Tell a Story

Another way to relax and focus on the people around you is to tell them a story. Use the story-telling format to sell yourself and your business, and include humorous experiences to make the story stand out and become memorable. Your story can take any form, be it advice, guidance, or education, but make sure it's laced with humor to keep it entertaining.

Pay Attention

A good communicator is also a good observer, so pay attention to finding something in common with the other person and use that to start a conversation. Don't present yourself as knowing it all, as this may be intimidating to some people, causing them to avoid you. And being a know-it-all is never attractive so let people join the debate before you kill it with your opinions.

Make the conversation about the other person rather than yourself. People will think you're arrogant and only want to show off if you put the spotlight on yourself. Make the conversation about how others will benefit from what you are saying, and you will notice that they will pay attention until you are finished.

Stop trying to be right, especially when dealing with someone you've just met. Being defensive and confrontational will destroy the relationship before it even begins.

Speak Properly and Clearly

People will judge you based on your speaking style, which is the first verbal expression they will receive from you. Your words and tone of your voice will be used to assess your leadership ability, cultural value, and intelligence. Mumbling is a sign of weakness. Instead, speak clearly to be heard. Combine your pitch with a flawless facial expression that shows what you're saying without hiding your intentions.

How to Master Small Talk to avoid Lacking What to Say

Isn't it amazing how some people can meet strangers and strike up a conversation that lasts for hours with no dull moments? They can accomplish this with a series of smaller conversations known as small talk.

Small talk will help you engage in a conversation with anyone without feeling awkward or making the person uncomfortable. Mastering the art of small talk will improve your networking skills, and you'll get to form lasting friendships.

Some people are antisocial, and no matter how much you try to compliment or question them, they will ignore you. Instead of feeling bad, bid them farewell and leave with a positive attitude. Just say, "All right, it was nice chatting with you. I'm off to meet my friends. I'll see you another time." If they aren't interested, let it go.

Small talk is intended to be uncontroversial and polite, so avoid discussing war, religion, politics, and similarly sensitive topics. Talking about such topics may end up increasing the distance between you two.

Certain in-depth discussions, such as those involving death, conspiracy theories, the end of the world, and those mentioned above, can make those around you feel uneasy. Avoid bringing up sensitive topics in the guise of small talk.

To keep the conversation going, build on your small talk or find related topics. For example, if you compliment someone's clothing and they appreciate it, you can ask where they purchased it or if you can order it online. Then you can move on to discussing matching shoes for such a dress, always leaving room for them to contribute more than you do in the conversation.

Drive the conversation, but let the other person keep it going with their opinion. Conversations are threads of related topics that can come from you or the other person. Be willing to listen to other people's stories.

Questions are excellent ways to learn new things but keep them relevant to the situation at hand. Digression from the topic could be interpreted as a lack of interest, and the other party may also become disinterested.

Instead of trying to sound interesting during small talk, be interested. Make it clear to the other person that you are paying attention to them. Small talk does not imply that you should entertain others by talking about yourself and other irrelevant topics; rather, you should be able to discuss related, friendly topics that are engaging for both parties.

You can ask emotional questions, such as what they like best about a city or your current environment. This should pique their interest enough so they will express themselves.

Pauses will happen, and it will be awkward. But don't be put off by them. Let them settle before speaking again. Don't force a conversation, no matter how much you want to say.

Finally, make small talk a habit. The only way to master this act is to practice with people on a bus, in a store, with colleagues, neighbors, and anyone else.

Tips for Introverts to Stay Engaged in Conversation

Conversations in a social setting begin with small talk and can progress to something deeper if both parties desire it.

When you first meet someone, it's not a good idea to bring up a personal subject like where they live and if they are in a relationship. The person you are speaking to could see your interest as too probing and uncomfortable.

Have a collection of conversation starters on hand, such as a compliment, a request, or asking random relatable questions, to use in various situations.

Asking them about themselves and their interests, connecting with any comments they make, and continuing the conversation with related topics are easy ways to move the conversation from its initial surface into a more meaningful territory.

Share a little of your vulnerability during conversions to encourage others to open up. For example, "I'm not very confident when it comes to puzzle games." This will prompt them to share one or two of their own vulnerabilities, but be careful not to scare people away with too much negativity.

To avoid social anxiety disorder, gradually expose yourself to social gatherings. Practice talking to people slowly, even if only for a few seconds at a time, and after a while of exchanging greetings, it will turn into a short conversation.

Start a friendship even if you're not sure they'll like you.

Express your emotions both verbally and non-verbally without considering the consequences. Just start the conversation, as the worst that can happen is that the person ignores you.

Group conversations can encourage you to be expressive, though you may struggle to get their attention. Raise your hands or make a gesture to get their attention, then begin speaking.

Being curious during a conversation will help you stay focused and interested. Introverts can easily zone out or become distracted during a conversation, but if you're curious, you'll be on the lookout for what the other person will say next.

Hacks to Help Deepen Initial Connection

Be genuine and honest. Don't try to fool others to impress them because you'll lose that connection the moment they figure it out.

Work out what is appropriate and what is not in social interactions. It's important to keep things light-hearted and avoid topics that could put the relationship at risk.

Pay attention and nod while the other person is speaking, as they need to know you're paying attention to them.

Share information about yourself that is not visible on the surface. This will give your connection a unique air of exclusivity.

Be aware and present as you communicate. Demonstrate compassion and open-mindedness without drama. There will be disagreements, but don't be dramatic about it.

Do things that demonstrate to others that you truly love and care about them.

When listening to others, be empathic. Listen to understand rather than to respond.

Spend quality time with your friends to strengthen your bonds and make more memories.

During a conversation, making eye contact shows that you are confident and interested in the subject.

All of this is topped off with a smile. A smile brightens the moods of others and allows them to relax and feel at ease in your presence.

Speaking with strangers or people you know isn't as difficult as it seems if you use small talk to put them at ease. A good two-way conversation is when you can express yourself and learn about others. Small talk will be required to initiate conversation, whether you are an extrovert or an introvert, especially with strangers.

The deaf rely so heavily on body language for expression and communication, so avoid sending mixed messages with your gestures and actions. As you put all of these tips and guidelines into action, keep a journal of your experiences so you can learn from your experiences to help you do better in the future.

Chapter 6: Instantly Master the Art of Storytelling

Did you know that storytelling is one of the oldest forms of communication? It's true. For centuries, people have been using stories to communicate ideas, values, and principles because stories can move people in a way that other methods can't.

People have been using stories to communicate ideas, values, and principles for centuries.
https://www.pexels.com/photo/photo-of-man-holding-pen-3182752/

It's no surprise that storytelling is back in fashion again. Everywhere you look, there are examples of brands using this technique to promote their products. But you may wonder, "How do I tell a story?" And more importantly, "What does it mean to tell a story?" While not everyone is born with the innate ability to tell stories that keep people on the edge of their seats, there are a few methods to develop and improve this ability. This chapter will explain everything you need to know about confidently telling a story, so read on to discover how!

What Is Storytelling?

Storytelling is simply the act of sharing a story from your life. Whether it's a funny anecdote or a challenging experience, the goal of storytelling is to connect with others by sharing your life experiences. The simplest and most effective form of storytelling is a first-person narrative, which involves you taking the role of the main character instead of retelling a story as if you were a spectator. It is an ancient art form that can be applied to almost any situation, whether in the classroom, at an event, or in the boardroom. It's an effective tool because it allows you to connect with an audience on a personal level by revealing aspects of your personality and providing examples of how you've applied your values in life. At the same time, it also allows you to relate to others by exposing common struggles and providing useful insights that can be applied to a variety of situations.

The Power of Storytelling to Develop Communication Skills

Are you someone who avoids eye contact, fidgets in a meeting, or speaks mostly about yourself? Then you're missing out on opportunities to build stronger relationships at work and socially. There are many ways to develop as a person and grow—but difficult conversations, team-building exercises, and insincere job interviews don't have to be among them. In fact, they can often be counterproductive. That's why so many people feel trapped in their comfort zone. Shyness, fear of saying the wrong thing, or fear of being misunderstood are all common roadblocks when it comes to communicating more authentically. A personal growth program can help make you comfortable enough to speak up and be yourself in any setting. However, it can also be as simple as adding storytelling as part of your communication skills toolkit —and here's why.

Storytelling is a powerful tool for developing communication skills because it forces you to slow down, analyze your feelings, and then constructively articulate them. By sharing a story, you're exploring your own feelings and bringing up a variety of emotions that may not have been present had you simply stated a fact or objective. This process can help you develop a more empathetic and authentic communication style. Storytelling is also a great tool for building trust, as it lets you peel back the layers of your personality and show your true self to others. By doing so, you can help others feel more comfortable communicating with you, as they're able to get a better sense of who you are and how you might respond in various situations.

How to Use Storytelling to Improve Your Communication Skills

It's easy to incorporate storytelling into your day-to-day life. You can use it when you're speaking to a friend or colleague, giving feedback to a direct report, or leading a meeting.

Here are a few ways you can use storytelling to enhance your communication skills:

- **Start with yourself** - First and foremost, you should begin by telling stories about yourself. This is especially important in the workplace, as you'll likely find that many of your colleagues are also hesitant to speak up. By sharing stories about your mistakes and successes, you can open up the conversation so that others will feel comfortable sharing as well

- **Share stories about a group** - Once you've become more comfortable sharing stories about yourself, you can start sharing stories about your team at work or your group of friends or family. This can help others feel more connected and make it easier to have difficult conversations by showing empathy and building trust. It can also help you identify areas where you may need to provide more guidance or coaching

- **Share stories about your clients** - If you work in a business-to-business setting, you can also use storytelling to help your clients feel more comfortable communicating with your company. Try sharing stories about clients who have struggled with a particular issue and how your company has addressed the challenge. This will help your clients feel at ease when communicating with your team and give them useful real-life examples they can apply to their own situations.

Why Storytelling Is an Effective Communication Tool

Storytelling is an effective communication tool because it helps you demonstrate empathy. By sharing a story, you're connecting with others by showing them the situations you've been in where you've struggled or succeeded. This will help others to not feel like they're alone and gives them a good example of how to deal with a similar situation in the future. In a workplace setting, it's common for people to feel they're in competition with one another rather than working toward a common goal. This can block collaboration and make it more challenging to work together toward a mutual outcome. By sharing a story about a previous experience or challenge, you can help others feel less alone and give them a better understanding of the pressures you face. This can help people feel like they can rely on you more and create a more collaborative environment.

Different Storytelling Styles: What's Your Style?

Let's say you are planning to narrate a story. Which style should you adopt? How can you make the story more interesting? Or, how can you make it more appealing to your listeners? A story is something that has a narrative, characters, and setting. However, not all stories are the same. There are different types of stories, and you can choose the type of story you want to tell depending on the situation. You can also mix and match them to get the best results.

Tell a Story That Makes People Laugh

Most of the time, the audience will be in a group setting, like a work environment or a social event. You can tell this story when you want people to feel good and have a great time together. You can use humor as a way to deal with some situations and make them more enjoyable. You don't need to be too serious with this type of story. You can make it a bit funny too. You can also use your own personal experience or an incident you happened to come across to tell a funny story. You can choose to tell a funny story at a wedding or any other event where you want people to be happy. A funny story will make your guests laugh and help them enjoy the event even more.

Tell a Dramatic Story

There are different types of stories, but some are more dramatic than others. A dramatic story could be about a tragedy you came across or an incident where there were a lot of conflicts, such as during a war. Dramatic stories are often about the unfairness of life and how humans struggle to cope with it. If you want to tell a dramatic story, you should find something that is interesting and meaningful. You can also choose to tell a dramatic story to help someone struggling with a situation they are facing or raise awareness about an issue.

Tell an Informative Story

An informative story provides information related to a topic, such as science, history, or the news. If you are planning to tell an informative story, you need to do some research first. You need to know what information you want to share with your audience. You can also use your own personal experience to tell an informative story. You can tell the story of how you experienced a situation or what you learned from it. You can also tell the story of how you overcame a challenge in your life. An informative story is helpful when you want to share information with your audience or your classmates, or you can even tell it on the radio or when you are narrating a video. An informative story can hold your audience's attention and make them interested in the topic you are talking about.

How to Tell a Story: The Art of Communicating Your Message

People love a good story. They're how we learn about each other and the world around us. There's nothing more enjoyable than being transported to a new place, time, or experience through the exchange of stories. Nurturing your ability to tell a story will help you connect with others on a deeper level and potentially open doors for you in your career and personal life. If you can find the perfect balance between brevity and detail, an anecdote helps your audience see the world from a new perspective. And with the right framework and structure, your story will have a lasting impact on your audience. By breaking down these principles into simple steps, you'll find it easier to communicate effectively as an individual or team member in any situation.

Know Your Audience

This may seem obvious, but knowing who you're speaking to and how they prefer to be engaged will help you tailor your story for maximum effect.

- **Professional:** In a professional setting, you'll have a better chance of being heard if you keep your story short and to the point. This means using only the information relevant to your point and leaving the rest out. If you're speaking at a conference or giving a keynote speech, you won't have the same amount of time to tell a story as you would in a one-on-one conversation. So, you'll need to be more concise and cut out all unnecessary chatter.

- **Social:** If you're in a more casual setting, you'll have more freedom to expand on your story and really paint a picture for your audience. Just remember that you still have a goal with this story. If you don't have a purpose for sharing it, then don't bother.

Hook 'Em with an Opener

This is your chance to get the full attention of your audience. You've got their attention with the topic, but now you want to hold onto it. One way to do this is to set up a sort of "trap" for your audience. By creating an expectation in your audience with a short phrase, you can surprise them with the rest of your story. A great example of this is a story about a man who has a hard time getting his car out of the driveway in the winter. The storyteller begins by saying, "When winter hits, and it's time to put your car away, there's one thing you need to remember: Don't forget to shovel the snow off your car!"

Establish Context

An old Japanese proverb says, "If you don't know where you are, you don't know who you are." Before you dive into the heart of your story, you want to give your audience a little context about where it takes place. This means finding a way to introduce the characters you are talking about and the specific situation or environment in which your story takes place. For example, if you're telling a story about the last time you went on vacation, you might want to give some context about who was there and what the weather was like. This will help your audience to picture themselves in this situation.

Tell the Main Event

The core of your story is what happened. It's the moment when everything changes, and you or your character is forced to adapt to a new situation they found themselves in. There are a few key things to keep in mind as you dive into this portion of the story:

- **Find the right balance between brevity and detail:** This means that you don't want to get too bogged down by the specifics of the event. It's not a play-by-play recall of everything that happened.
- **Focus on the main character of the story:** Who was involved in the event? What role did they play? What is the character's relationship to your audience? You want to bring this character to life for your audience.
- **Take responsibility for the event:** Your main event should be presented as something that happened to you and not something that "just happened."
- **Use concrete details to paint a picture for your audience:** By using specific examples and details, you help your audience to fully immerse themselves in the story.

Wrap up with a Conclusion

This is where you take everything that happened in your story and apply it to the lesson you want your audience to walk away with. There are a few different ways to go about this. You can tie the story back to a specific person, idea, or feeling. Or, you can walk the audience through the steps you took to come out on top. Whatever you decide to do, your conclusion should feel like a natural extension of the story. You don't want to end up with a conclusion that feels abrupt or forced.

Keep these three things in mind when crafting your conclusion:

1. **Be clear:** You want your conclusion to be unmistakable. It can't be open to interpretation. It needs to be clear and direct.
2. **Be concise:** You don't want to ramble on and on until your audience starts to lose interest. Make your point and move on.
3. **Keep it positive:** While it's crucial to learn from your mistakes, your conclusion should be more about what you learned and less about the "wrong" things that happened.

Exercises for Better Storytelling

While you can't force everyone to listen, you can prepare yourself to share stories that elicit a particular reaction by practicing techniques that help you to feel more confident sharing stories.

Here are a few tips to help you become a better storyteller:

- **Choose a story that resonates with you** - The first thing you should do when preparing to share a story is to think about which stories resonate with you the most. This could be a challenging experience you've faced or an anecdote that makes you laugh. Once you've decided which story you'd like to share, ask yourself why it resonates with you. This will help you prepare for the conversation and make it easier for you to transition from the story back to the present.

- **Understand the story** - This doesn't mean you have to memorize the entire story, but you should try to understand the main point and how it applies to the conversation at hand. This will help you transition seamlessly from the story back to the present and provide others with a better understanding of what you're trying to say. Try keeping a journal and writing down anything out of the ordinary that happens to you or someone else. This will make your storytelling feel more realistic.

- **Connect with your audience** - Once you've shared the story, try to make eye contact with as many people in the room as possible. This will help you engage with your audience and show that you're connected with them and the story. This can also help you identify any questions or concerns that the audience may have so you can address them effectively.

Here are some tips to help you become more comfortable sharing stories:

- **Pick a few stories** - Before you jump into a conversation, try to think about the stories that you'd like to share. This helps you prepare for the conversation and makes it easier to transition from the story back to the present. You can try picking a few stories which address challenges your team is facing and how you're working to overcome them. Alternatively, you can search YouTube for comedians or podcasters and use their storytelling abilities as inspiration.

- **Prepare yourself** - Before you hop into the conversation, try to get yourself in the right mindset. This may mean taking a few deep breaths, meditating, or practicing a breathing exercise. Alternatively, you can try thinking about the examples you're going to share and how they apply to your team. This will help you stay focused during the conversation and keep you from getting overwhelmed by the attention.
- **Practice makes perfect** - Once you've committed to becoming a more confident storyteller, practice. This doesn't mean you have to memorize the story by heart, but you can try to get used to sharing it in conversations. The outcome will mean you are more comfortable speaking up, and this will make it easier for you to transition from the story back to the present.

Communicating your message effectively is an art form. It's not something that comes naturally to everyone, but it can be learned and improved with practice. If you're looking to become a better storyteller, try putting yourself in situations where you have to tell a story. Whether that's at a family gathering or in the office, you'll find that it's a great way to improve your communication skills. When all is said and done, a well-told story can capture any audience, be it with friends, over a beer, or with colleagues in a meeting. Just remember to know your audience, establish context, tell the main event, and wrap up with a conclusion, and you'll be well on your way to becoming a better storyteller.

Chapter 7: 15 Tips to Communicate in Groups Effortlessly

Communication is one of the most important skills you can have. It's also something that many people struggle with, especially in a group setting.

Communication is one of the most important skills you can have
https://www.pexels.com/photo/colleagues-shaking-each-other-s-hands-3184291/

When speaking with just one other person, we are able to clearly express our thoughts and get our message across. However, once there are more than two people involved, things get much trickier.

In group settings, it's easy to feel left out or overlooked when everyone else seems to be getting along so well. Because of this, being able to communicate effectively within a group setting is a very useful skill to have.

If you find yourself struggling with communication in group settings, read on for some helpful tips to change your social dynamic for the better!

Why Communicating within a Group Setting Can Be Difficult

When working in a large team or out with a group of friends, the ability to communicate clearly and effectively is crucial. Unfortunately, these are skills not everyone possesses. In any group environment, there is a risk that communication will be stifled by shyness, antagonism, or introversion. People have their own personalities and life experiences that can make communication difficult.

And let's face it - not everyone is great at making small talk. As much as we all love getting to know new people, most of us would prefer if group settings were a little less awkward. We all want to be that person who makes those around us feel comfortable and at ease. But when you're in a situation where you don't know anyone, it can be hard to break the ice. If you struggle with building rapport with new people, it's probably because you're not speaking their language or you don't understand theirs. Most people are more likely to open up and trust someone who has an interest in similar things or who understands their interests. Our ability to make friends and build rapport with those around us is directly related to our communication skills. Whether you're an introverted individual or simply someone who struggles to meet new people, learning the ins and outs of communication is part of feeling more confident and capable. With this in mind, here are some communication tips for group settings that will help you make friends and build rapport with everyone around you.

Prevent Others from Talking over You

It can be extremely frustrating if you're in a situation where people keep interrupting you. It is disrespectful and can make it difficult to feel comfortable and build a rapport with people. If you notice that people are interrupting you, there are some things you can do to stop this and prevent others from talking over you.

- First of all, try to make eye contact with the person who is interrupting you and give them a slight nod or a head tilt to let them know that you're ready for them to speak. This will help them realize that you've not finished talking yet.

- You can also use non-verbal cues to try and get the attention of the person who is interrupting you. Folding your arms, for example, can send a signal that you need to finish what you're saying.

Communicate Clearly

Communication is the transfer of information between people so that they can understand each other. The clearer you are in your conversation, the quicker and more effectively you will be able to convey your message, and the less chance there is of causing confusion or misunderstanding. You can increase clarity in your interaction by using simple language, making eye contact, and asking questions.

- Write down your ideas and thoughts before you communicate them. This helps you to organize your thoughts and choose the right words to express yourself effectively.

- Make sure you're looking directly at the person you're communicating with. This will show them that you're focused on what they're saying and that you're engaged and interested.

- Ask questions if you're not sure the person understands what you're saying. This will also show that you're engaged and interested in what they have to say.

Confirm Understanding

While you should also work to ensure that you fully understand the other person's message, it's also worth bearing in mind that you don't want to put words in someone else's mouth. To avoid this, you can use a few key phrases like "I think what you're trying to say is..." or "Does this mean...?" to confirm that you fully understand their message. This can help avoid misunderstandings between you and the other person and reinforce that you're actively listening. By confirming that you understand, you'll also make the other person feel more confident in your abilities as a communicator. This will also make you look more professional and capable, which will be beneficial in the long run.

Attract Attention

If you're in a group setting and want to get someone's attention, be aware of how you're doing it. By simply raising your hand, you may come across as aggressive, whereas by waving your hand, you're being more

receptive.
- If you want to attract the attention of someone who is sitting across from you at a table, you can use the palm-up wave. This is considered a receptive gesture.
- If you want to attract the attention of someone who is sitting beside you, you can use the palm-down wave, which is considered more aggressive.
- Another way to attract attention in a group setting is by using non-verbal sounds. If you want to call attention from someone who is on your left, for example, you can use a "tsk" sound with your tongue to get their attention.
- Be opinionated. In a group, its members tend to direct their communicative attention more to people who have stronger opinions, as the article "Interpersonal communication in small groups" published in the Journal of Abnormal and Social Psychology shows.

Be Mindful of Body Language

Your body language can have a huge impact on your communication. If you're hunched over, crossing your arms, and avoiding eye contact, people will see you as closed-off and uninterested in what they have to say. While you should always be mindful of how you present yourself, it can be particularly useful when you're communicating with a large group of people. If the majority of your team sits at the back of the office and you sit at the front, it will send out a very different impression. Taking care of your body language will give off a much more confident and engaging impression and make communication much easier.

Communication Works Both Ways

Communication is a two-way street, and it's essential to ensure that you're actively listening to the other people in your group. While you should be mindful of the people speaking and actively listening, you should also be checking in with the rest of the group. This can help to avoid any one-on-one discussions getting out of hand or becoming distractions, but it can also help you avoid putting your foot in it. If you notice that a few people are looking frustrated or disengaged, you can use this as an opportunity to check in with the group as a whole. By actively checking in with the rest of the group, you can identify potential issues and repair any damaged relationships before they become serious problems.

Take Control

If you're new to the group or want to steer a conversation to a particular topic, ensuring you have control over the conversation can help you build rapport with others. If you have to take control of the conversation, doing so abruptly can be uncomfortable for other people and will make it harder to build rapport. Instead, try bridging into the topic with a question. Asking a question is a great way to steer a conversation and lead it to a particular topic that you want to discuss. If you're nervous about taking control of the conversation, you can start with a general question that everyone can contribute to.

Watch Your Vocabulary

You might be tempted to use big and impressive words to sound like you know what you're talking about. However, this can backfire and make you sound less intelligent. You should watch your vocabulary in a few different ways:

- Avoid using jargon or industry-specific language where possible. Unless you're talking to other members of your team or in a meeting, this can make you sound like you're trying to show off, and if used incorrectly, it makes you seem like a complete fool.

- Make sure that the words you use are appropriate for the person you're talking to. If they're not a scientist, don't talk to them like they are! This may sound obvious, but it can easily be overlooked.

- Avoid using words that may be considered offensive or using offensive phrases. You never know what other people's backgrounds and experiences are and the last thing you want to do is make someone feel uncomfortable or offend anyone.

Ask Questions and Be an Active Listener

Active listening will help you communicate better by building trust between you and the person you're speaking to, so you can understand where they're coming from. If you're speaking with someone and want to help them open up, asking questions is a great way to do so. You can use open-ended questions, which are questions that can't be answered with a yes or no. You can also ask them if they want to share a story. This can be helpful if the other person is someone you look up to or admire.

Eye Contact and Body Language

Did you know that communication happens more than verbally? In fact, non-verbal communication accounts for at least two-thirds of the communication process. When you're in a group setting, you want to focus on eye contact and other non-verbal cues as you normally would in one-on-one communication. Eye contact is sometimes seen as intimidating when you're speaking to one other person, but it's important in a group setting because it helps you connect with others and build rapport with them. When communicating with others, you want to be aware of a handful of things. Your posture says a lot about you, and you want to make sure that it's open and inviting. You also want to ensure you're not blocking anyone from the conversation or actively forcing them to look away from you. Be aware of your hands and make sure that they're not blocking someone out or that they are being used aggressively.

Use Small Talk

Small talk is simply the casual and informal exchange of superficial remarks. When you're in a new group setting, the best way to begin is by asking questions related to the event or the surroundings.

- If you're at a networking event, you may ask who some people are and what they do.
- If you're at a wedding, you may ask who is married to whom and how long they've been together.
- At a conference or lecture, you could ask what the speakers are most excited about and what people are excited about in the industry.
- You can also ask about the group and if anyone knows each other.
- You want to be sure to ask open-ended questions. These types of questions invite deeper and more interesting responses from the group. Closed-ended questions are more likely to result in short, surface-level answers and no further conversation.

Tell Stories

Stories are one of the most effective ways to create a connection with those around you. There are many types of stories that you can tell in a group setting to help you build a connection.

- If you're at a wedding and know that the bride is a huge sports fan, instead of asking about her career, you could ask about her favorite sports team, and then you could share a story about one of your favorite games and teams.
- If you're at a networking event and know that the person you're talking to is hoping to get a promotion soon, instead of asking about the company or their job, you could ask about their career, and then you could share a story about your experience with promotions and the best ways to earn them.

Establish Commonalities

If you've been talking with a group of people for a while and have established some rapport, you can try to discover commonalities that exist between you and the group. The goal here is to discover what people are most passionate about in their lives and work. People tend to be more engaged and excited when talking about the things they enjoy.

Use Humor

Humor is a great way to break the ice and make a lasting connection with the people around you. If you're unsure about making small talk and breaking the ice with a group, try using humor to help you get started. You can try to bring humor into your questions or stories or use it in a self-deprecating way. Self-deprecation involves making light of your own flaws and mistakes in a self-aware way that is meant to make you less serious and less intimidating. You may notice that the people around you are hesitant to speak up or ask questions. If this is the case, using humor can help you break the ice and encourage everyone to feel more comfortable speaking up.

Share Things about Yourself

This is a great tip to remember when building rapport with almost any group. People want to know if you've done things in your life that you're proud of. Share your achievements and the other things in your life that you're proudest of. You might be at a wedding and be proud of graduating from university or getting a promotion at work. You may be at a networking event and be proud of starting your own business or receiving an award for your work. Depending on the group, you may also want to share your passions and interests. You can do this by mentioning what you're most excited about in your life, and be sure to mention the things that you've achieved.

Practical Exercises

To help you get started with group communication, here are the essential components you need to work on the next time you find yourself in a group setting.

Make Yourself Heard

Instead of letting feelings build up inside, be the one to speak up and express what you're feeling.

Another advantage of speaking up is that it allows other people to speak up too. By listening attentively and respectfully, everyone can feel included in the conversation. Nobody should feel as though they're being left out. By speaking up, you are doing your part to create a positive environment for everyone to feel comfortable enough to share their feelings. Speaking up also creates a sense of accountability, which helps keep people on track with their goals and keeps them accountable to each other.

Finally, speaking up helps to show that you respect yourself. How can you expect others to do so if you don't value your own thoughts and feelings? By speaking up and expressing yourself, you demonstrate that you respect yourself enough to listen to what you have to say. So, make sure that you acknowledge people as they speak, ask questions when appropriate, and listen carefully to what others are saying.

Be Prepared for Different Answers

One of the biggest challenges for anyone is knowing how to get the most out of it. How do you know what is going on? What should you be looking for? How can you best contribute to the discussion? One of the keys to successfully navigating a group discussion is to be prepared. This means being ready to respond when asked questions or making comments of your own. In addition: Be aware that different people will have different perceptions. Don't be afraid to disagree with someone's opinion or diverge from the group consensus if you feel strongly about it. But don't get too far off track by trying to argue against everyone else, either. Remember that people are allowed to have their own opinions as long as they are respectful and considerate when expressing them.

Empathize

Empathy is the ability to understand and share another person's feelings. Empathetic listening means taking a moment to put yourself in someone else's shoes. For example, imagine how it feels to be frustrated by a long commute or how scary it must be to have cancer. Empathetic listening is especially necessary when you're talking with people who may be experiencing difficult emotions. It can help you recognize their needs and show that you care about them.

There are many ways to listen with empathy:

- **Listen actively**. Avoid distractions like checking your phone or multitasking. Instead, focus on what the other person is saying and try to understand where they're coming from.
- **Be open-minded and nonjudgmental**. Don't assume that people will automatically agree with your point of view, but don't ignore their opinions either — take them into account when making your own decisions.
- **Show empathy through your tone of voice**. Speak clearly and calmly without getting defensive or sarcastic. If you find yourself becoming frustrated, try pausing before answering or try another approach (such as asking questions or paraphrasing).

Communication is not just about saying the words that come out of your mouth. It is an entire process that includes how you behave, make eye contact, and tone of your voice. If you want to make friends and build a rapport with people in a group setting, communicate using eye contact and body language. Use small talk to learn about the group and the things they are interested in. Tell stories, discover commonalities, and finally, be confident and proud of yourself and your achievements. Most importantly, be yourself and remember that building rapport is about being comfortable with people, so don't try too hard to be something you're not.

Chapter 8: Become an Amazing Public Speaker

Public speaking is a skill that many people fear and do everything they can to avoid. This fear can often inhibit the career prospects of even the most talented individuals. The National Institutes of Mental Health found that 75 percent of people fear public speaking. Some people fear it because of how many different audiences they may address (e.g., large groups). Others are terrified by the thought of giving a speech or talking to a single person who wields power over them, such as their supervisor, interviewer, and professor, during an oral exam.

Public speaking is a skill that many people fear and do everything they can to avoid.
https://www.pexels.com/photo/man-beside-flat-screen-television-with-photos-background-716276/

Public speaking can be a challenging undertaking. Nervousness is a part of life, and being nervous about public speaking is no exception. Some people are naturally gifted speakers and can command an audience with ease. For those who aren't, it takes time, practice, and patience to improve their skills. Public speaking is like riding a bike. You can only do it if you get on and start pedaling. You may be surprised at how much easier it is to speak in front of people when you know what to expect.

The following is a guide to help you understand the process of public speaking and how to overcome your fears. It's vital that you approach the task with an open mind and leave any preconceived ideas behind. There is no right or wrong way to do it as long as you are honest with yourself and your audience.

Lack of Confidence

You'll risk alienating the audience if you don't have confidence in yourself and the topic you're talking about. A confident speaker connects with the audience and makes them feel like they're part of the discussion. If you're not confident, it will show in your body language and the way you speak. You may struggle to make eye contact with your audience or struggle to stay on topic. You may also be tempted to use filler words like "um" and "ah," making it sound like you're not sure of what you're saying. To build self-confidence in public speaking, you should identify and address what causes your lack of confidence. Here are some of the common causes:

Preparation

A good public speaker is always prepared. Even if you're not a naturally confident person, you can still build self-confidence as a public speaker by preparing yourself adequately. Come up with an outline of what you want to say, and practice it several times before giving your speech. This will help you avoid making mistakes or forgetting what comes next in your presentation. You should also practice reading your speech aloud. This will help you get used to speaking in front of an audience, which is a key part of building self-confidence as a public speaker.

Visualization

Visualization is a technique that helps you get comfortable with the idea of public speaking. To use it, imagine yourself giving your speech and seeing yourself succeed. Try to picture as many details as possible. How are people responding? Are they laughing at your jokes? Can you see them nodding their heads in agreement? Imagine every aspect of the situation, including how you feel while delivering the speech. This will help you get used to what it will be like when you actually give the presentation.

Self-Talk

A lot of people have negative thoughts about public speaking. These can include things like "I'm going to mess up" or "Everyone will think I'm stupid for saying this." If you have these thoughts, try replacing them with more positive ones. Replace the thought "I'm going to mess up" with "No one will notice if I make a mistake. It happens all the time at presentations, and no one minds." This technique is called self-talk because it involves talking yourself through the situation using positive affirmations instead of negative statements.

Confidence follows action. The more you try something and succeed, the more confident you will be in that particular skill. For example, playing a musical instrument. At first, your fingers fumble, and you're embarrassed to make mistakes in front of others—but with practice, you grow more confident and soon learn how to play well enough so that other people enjoy listening. To become confident as a speaker, it is essential that you practice regularly in front of other people. Practice in front of a mirror or on video. You need to be able to see yourself speaking so that you can notice when you are making mistakes and learn from them.

Lack of Attention to the Audience

To be a successful public speaker, you need to know your audience. Maybe you are aware that some members of your audience might be hostile to or skeptical about what you're proposing. You may be confident in your ability as a speaker but worry that your audience may not relate to you. You can eliminate the disconnection by identifying the gaps and tackling them accordingly.

For example, if you are speaking about a new type of software for business owners and your audience includes executives who are not technically adept, it may be helpful to provide more details than you would otherwise. If your talk is aimed at entrepreneurs, but some of your audience members work in large companies that aren't likely to use the product you're promoting, they may appreciate hearing how they can help their firms benefit from what you're proposing. While you can't always predict what your audience will need, you should at least make an effort to account for it. The following are some tips to help you identify the needs of your listeners:

Research the Audience

You've probably heard the old adage that "a little knowledge is a dangerous thing," and it's especially true when you're speaking. Researching your audience can help you tailor your talk so it meets their needs rather than simply pushing your own agenda. It also gives you a chance to make sure that whatever point of view you have on a subject does line up with theirs. If there are any major differences between what they think and what you do, those differences should be addressed during the presentation rather than just ignored. One of the best ways to research your audience is through surveys. Surveys can be as simple as an email or paper survey you send out before an event, or they can be more elaborate and include a website where people can post comments about their ideas on a subject. When preparing to speak at an event, consider what your audience might want and need from the talk.

Researching your audience beforehand will help you to engage with them more personally and make your speech more interesting. You should also try to understand what motivates your audience. If you can figure out what drives them, finding common ground with them and speaking a language they understand will be easier.

Hook Your Audience Fast

The hook is the first thing you say or do to grab your audience's attention. It should be a simple statement that makes an immediate connection with your audience and shows them what they can expect from you during the speech. The hook should also be brief, memorable, and relevant to your audience. You can use a rhetorical question, quote a well-known person or authority on the subject, or tell a quick anecdote that illustrates what you'll be discussing in more detail later.

Tell a Compelling Story

One of the most effective ways to make your audience listen is by telling a compelling story as you have read previously. It doesn't have to be an elaborate story full of plot twists and turns, but it should be an interesting and engaging one that makes your audience want to hear more. A great story can be used as a hook to get the audience's attention or woven throughout your speech. You can also use it to illustrate a point or reinforce an idea.

Lack of Preparedness

Before giving a speech, practice it in its entirety. Doing so allows you to hear where you are rushing or mumbling words and also allows your voice intonation and enthusiasm levels to feel natural. Using visuals, technology, or other aids beforehand also makes it possible to catch and eliminate glitches in the presentation. Rehearsal prepares speakers to be more familiar with their material so they can field questions effectively. Your speech will be filled with stumbles and awkward pauses when you don't practice. You may lose your place in the text and need to turn pages or notes. The audience will see that you are nervous and uncomfortable, which doesn't inspire confidence in your message. To be better prepared before the speech, you should do the following:

Gather Early Feedback

The best way to prepare for your speech is to talk about it with others. They can provide feedback on your presentation's content, delivery, and style. Ask them if they understand what you are trying to communicate and whether anything is confusing or missing from your message. You should also ask them if they think the speech is interesting and whether it will hold the audience's attention. Ask them how they would improve or change your presentation. You may need to rewrite some parts or add details to keep people engaged and interested in what you are saying.

Use Your Voice and Body Language

Your voice and body language are two of the most powerful tools in your arsenal as a speaker. Use them to convey passion, enthusiasm, and emotion. Use the tone of your voice to emphasize important points and create excitement in your speech. A low or monotone voice can make you sound boring and uninterested in what you're saying. A high-pitched voice may make you sound too emotional – *as if every word is a big deal.* Find a happy medium where your voice has energy but doesn't go up and down like an elevator, as this will help keep your audience engaged.

Use body language to project confidence and authority even if you feel nervous or unsure. Stand up straight, smile, look at the audience while speaking, gesture with open palms when appropriate, and avoid fidgeting with things such as pens or papers on the podium. In one study, students who sat upright—as opposed to slouching—exuded more confidence and felt more confident about themselves. Walking confidently will let the audience know you have something valuable to share in your presentation. Use gestures to emphasize important points and create excitement in your speech.

For instance, you can use your hands to emphasize a point or gesture toward something in the audience. If you're talking about a new product available on your company's website, point to the URL on an overhead projector so people can see it. This will make them feel as though they can relate to and engage with the topic.

Listen to Yourself When You Speak

It may sound silly, but it's easy to get lost in your words and not hear yourself. While practicing, listen for awkward pauses or sounds that don't flow well with the rest of your sentence. If someone makes a comment during your speech, listen to the tone of their voice and how they phrase what they say. This will help you understand how others are receiving what you have to say just as much as it helps them understand you!

Lack of Time Management

Always run through the speech before you deliver it. This is how you iron out any kinks in the wording, and it gives you time to practice reading at the right speed. Speakers often run overtime because they aren't adequately prepared and can't get through their material in the allotted time. If you tend to run late, set the alarm on your watch or phone to go off five minutes before the end of your talk. Make sure it's in your pocket and set to silent mode. The vibrations will let you know when it's time to wrap things up. A good rule of thumb is to practice concluding your speech two minutes before the timer goes off. This gives you the time to catch up if you're slacking off or an audience member asks a question.

Overcoming Stage Fright

Stage fright can be a very uncomfortable experience. It can take over your thoughts, making it hard for you to concentrate on anything else. It can also affect your body and make you feel sick or tense. As well as being a very unpleasant experience, it can also be very damaging to your performance. Stage fright can be tough to overcome, but there are some things you can do.

Get in the Right Mindset

The first thing you need to do is get into the right mindset. Don't think of stage fright as an illness but rather as a normal human response. You're not alone in having these feelings, and it's okay for them to happen. They are very common feelings to performers. The more you think of stage fright as a normal response, the easier it will be to manage. Try not to think of yourself as a performer and instead just be in the moment. This can help you get over any feelings of anxiety or fear.

Try writing down your thoughts and feelings before you go on stage, so you have time to process them. You may find that your thoughts and feelings aren't as bad as you thought.

Belly Breathe

Belly Breathing is a great way to calm your nerves. It's a technique that will help you slow down and focus on the present moment, which can help prevent any feelings of anxiety or fear from taking over. To do this exercise:

1. Take a deep breath through your nostrils and let it out through your mouth.
2. Repeat this process three times.
3. Once you've completed three rounds of belly breathing, take a moment to focus on how your body feels. You may find that it's easier to relax and focus on the task at hand.

Greet Your Audience and Smile

The hardest part is to initiate the speech —and that's why you should start by greeting your audience. It's a simple but effective way to start the speech off on the right footing and can help put you at ease. When you enter the room, smile and look out at everyone in your audience, take a moment to think about what they want from this presentation, as it can make all the difference when it comes time to deliver your message.

Turn the Spotlight Around

When you're in a spotlight—whether that spotlight is bright, dim, or just flickering on and off—it can make you feel as though everyone else sees more of your flaws than they do when you're not on stage. So turn the attention around. Now it's on others rather than yourself. You can ask questions that involve the audience or share stories they can relate to. If you're giving a presentation on building a kitchen island, ask people what kind of island they would like to see in their home. That way, you'll turn the spotlight onto them and allow them to share their thoughts and ideas with one another—and with you.

Move!

If you're feeling nervous, it's easy to get locked into one position: standing in front of the audience, behind your podium. Movement helps to keep you focused and breaks up the monotony of standing still. Try moving around the stage periodically as you speak; this will give your audience a chance to see different angles and perspectives on what you're saying. If you're too nervous about moving on your own, try moving when someone in the audience asks a question or makes a comment. This can effectively keep the interaction going without having to come up with something new to say.

Pause Occasionally

Pausing occasionally while talking lets your audience digest what they have just heard – and provides an opportunity for them to ask questions. It will also give you a chance to catch your breath, which can be particularly handy if you're feeling nervous and need to take a moment before continuing. The best time to pause is after making a major point or when you've said something particularly important. Make sure you look at the audience while pausing, as this will help them follow what you're saying.

Picture the Audience Naked

One of the oldest tricks to overcome stage fright is to picture the audience naked. This will make them seem less intimidating and more approachable. This technique takes the pressure off you and puts it on the audience. You'll realize they can't be too critical or judgmental about what you say if they're naked. They'll just be people like everyone else! If you can't picture the audience naked, try imagining that they're wearing unflattering costumes. Maybe they're dressed as clowns or superheroes, or maybe their clothes are on backward. This will help you see them in a new light and make them less intimidating.

Public Speaking Exercises

Vocal Warmups

Vocal warmups are often associated with musicians, but they can help public speakers too. These exercises help ease tension and warm up your voice, so it's ready for public speaking. Try these vocal warmups before you get on stage:

- Humming
- Singing scales (for singers)
- Repeating vowel sounds to loosen your facial muscles

Although most public speakers do not need to hit particular notes while speaking, it is still a good idea for them to warm up.

Talking to the Mirror

One of the most effective public speaking practices is talking to a mirror. This can be done in front of a full-length mirror – or one positioned at an angle so that you can look at yourself from your audience's perspective. The point of this exercise is to look at yourself while speaking and see if you are making any physical movements that may distract your audience. If you are making gestures with your hands, try to keep them subtle by making smaller movements or only using one hand at a time. You can also practice smiling in the mirror so that you know how it will look when you are presenting.

Try Eliminating the Fillers

Filler words are "um" and "ah"—words that don't add value to what you're saying. Try this exercise to eliminate filler words from your speech patterns. Speak for as long as you can without using any of these words. If you find yourself using them, stop and start again.

Pick up an Object and Talk about It

This technique will help you to feel more comfortable talking about unfamiliar topics or improvising on the spot. Set up a timer for five minutes, pick a random object and talk about it. You'll find it surprisingly difficult. However, it will become second nature with practice. Combine it with the "Try Eliminating the Fillers" exercise for better results. This exercise comes in handy when dealing with the numerous unknown variables on-stage, like an audience member asking a question you don't know the answer to or the slides suddenly going blank.

Chapter 9: How to Manage an Argument Like a Boss

Arguments are a part of any relationship, whether it be romantic, platonic, or strictly professional. As long as we aren't clones of each other, there are always going to be misunderstandings and disagreements between different people. Arguments are impossible to prevent altogether, but we can navigate through them productively and gracefully.

Arguments are a part of any relationship, whether it be romantic, platonic, or strictly professional.
https://www.pexels.com/photo/worried-couple-with-notebook-looking-at-each-other-4246239/

It's difficult to deal with conflict and resolve it peacefully, but it's also an incredibly valuable skill. Whether volatile, destructive emotions cloud your judgment or you're non-confrontational to the extreme, know that arguments don't have to be so stressful to handle. An argument is an opportunity to understand another person and strengthen your bond as a result.

Learning how to have a productive argument is a matter of practice, but first, you need to learn what that looks like. We don't get many examples of what a healthy argument looks like in our lives, but it is possible for you to make it the norm for your relationships. As you read on, actively reflect on your own behavior and how you can better your conflict resolution skills.

Understanding What Happens During an Argument

The words exchanged during an argument only scratch the surface of what's going on. There's an underlying structure to all verbal disagreements. We don't tend to notice it when we're in the heat of the moment, so see how these elements can be applied to arguments you've had. Here's a concrete example.

Charlotte is Emma's younger sister, and they live together in Emma's apartment. One day when she was out of the city due to work, Emma called Charlotte and told her to clean up the apartment. "I'll be receiving a very important client at our place, so it absolutely has to be spotless. They're a difficult person to please and kind of a germaphobe. I'm very stressed about this, so please make it presentable."

Charlotte had several tests to study for, but she postponed her studying to help her sister out. She then pulled an all-nighter to catch up with her studies. After Emma received her client, she went to Charlotte's room and told her, "I can't believe you would do this to me, Charlotte! When I came home, the TV was still dusty, and the client complained about it to me. I was so embarrassed! I know you had other things to do, but my job is what pays for our apartment."

Charlotte was quick to defend herself, "That just sounds like they were looking for things to be upset about! I did forget to wipe the TV clean, but everything else was spotless, wasn't it?"

But Emma wouldn't have any of it. "I don't know why it's so difficult for you to accept when you're wrong. You messed up, and there's nothing to really argue about. I don't even know if taking you was the right choice now."

Feeling defeated and not wanting to upset her sister any further, Charlotte just apologized and left. This argument was completely unproductive, and it put a strain on the sisters' relationship for weeks afterward. To really understand what happened here, we'll look at each argument as if it was made up of smaller arguments.

What Really Happened?

Most arguments break out because the involved parties disagree on what happened. Whose story is right? Was it really Charlotte's job to deep-clean the entire apartment? Was Emma throwing her weight around as the breadwinner to intimidate her sister? Whose responsibility is the upkeep of the apartment?

The Objective Truth; Who's Right?

During arguments, people get too hung up on who's "objectively correct" and immediately jump to try to convince the other party that they're right. Arguments aren't really about facts. Both Charlotte and Emma agreed that the TV was dusty. What they didn't agree on was whether it was such a big deal. Arguments are about conflicting perceptions, and there's no clear-cut "right or wrong" judgment we can pass on those.

What to Do About It

Free yourself from the impossible task of determining who's really in the right. Even if you could, that's not what the argument is about. When you're confronted with the need to make this judgment, think about the true facts and whether you disagree with the facts or your perception of them.

Refrain from stating your feelings and perception as "the truth." They may be your truth, but they're not a universal truth. Each party brings its own perceptions to the table. You most likely have a lot to learn from the other person, and they have a lot to learn from you too. Focus on looking at the argument from the other person's point of view and try to understand how they saw it.

Intent; Why Did They Say That?

A person's intentions greatly influence what we think about them, despite the final result of their actions. Whether or not someone thinks badly of you will also influence how an argument with them will go. Did Charlotte not give enough importance to Emma's plea? Did Emma mention that she was unsure of her decision to take Charlotte in because she wanted to subtly threaten her, to make a point, or did she just say that in the heat of the moment?

The number one mistake we make here is that we assume we know what someone's intentions are. In fact, we can't know. As humans, we have to do this to some extent, but it's gone too far when someone's imaginary intent is derailing an entire conversation.

People may act with good intentions yet still cause irreparable damage. They may act with mixed intentions for reasons unknown even to them. They may have bad intentions that we're unaware of. According to a study, intentions explain about 28% of the variance in future behavior.

What to Do About It

Be aware that you can't know what's going through the other person's head. People show their intentions through actions, but what may be clear and obvious to you may be total conjecture to someone else.

Rather than intent, focus on impact. Find out how your words impacted the other person, and let them know how their words impacted you. Ask them what they were thinking at that moment and whether their impact lined up with what they really meant to say.

The Blame Game; Whose Fault Is It?

Nobody likes to be burdened with blame. People will go to great lengths to not be burdened with blame, putting a lot more on the line than you'd think. Nobody likes to blame, not only because it doesn't feel good but also because they don't feel it's all their fault. The truth is that it really isn't.

Charlotte thought that she was asked to drop everything to help Emma on short notice, and she did her part, so she's not to blame. Emma thought that since Charlotte took on the responsibility of cleaning the apartment, she was to blame if it wasn't done perfectly.

As a third party, it's easy to see how each girl contributed to the problem. When we're participants, emotions run high, and it's not easy to admit mistakes. Talking about blame is not only useless, but it's a surefire way to anger the other party even more.

What to Do About It

When you think in "It's them or me" terms, you miss the bigger picture. It's not all your fault, and it's not all their fault. Instead of trying to get the "guilty" party to admit blame, understand that the argument took place between two people. Both of you contributed to it in different ways.

What Do I Do with All These Feelings?

Feelings are always messy. Unfortunately, arguments between people are almost always about feelings. When feelings come up in an argument, people almost always shy away from them because feelings cloud your objective judgment.

Openly showing your feelings can lead people to believe that you're too emotional or that you're too sensitive. For many of us, wearing your heart on your sleeve is risky. When you've been burned before, openly showing your vulnerabilities like we ought to show our feelings feels silly.

What if you get brushed off? What if your feelings hurt someone that you didn't intend to hurt? And are we ready to face what the other person feels about us? This is why people are wary of getting into the feeling's territory during arguments.

As messy as feelings are, you have to dive into them if you want to solve a nasty argument. "I'm very stressed about this, so please make it presentable" shows Emma's anxiety, frustration, and restlessness. "That just sounds like they were looking for things to be upset about," shows Charlotte's disbelief, hurt, and annoyance. These feelings were the crux of the argument, yet they were never discussed.

If you're someone who gets carried away by feelings of anger and hurt during an argument, bombarding the other person with them is also not the solution. Despite what the other person might have done to provoke you, your feelings are your responsibility. It's not right to unfairly barrage someone with your feelings, no matter what.

What to Do About It

First of all, you don't have to react to the first thing you feel. If your immediate reaction to someone's words is anger, you don't have to show it straight away. Take a few seconds to reflect and debate whether it'll steer the conversation in the right direction if you react with anger.

Before determining what you'll be doing in the future or how you'll be fixing the problem, there should be a conversation about feelings. Express yourself calmly and rationally, and let the other person express their feelings. Listen without judgment, and acknowledge that their feelings are as real as yours.

What Does This Say about Who I Am?

As we argue with someone else on the outside, we're having our own little argument on the inside too. Arguing with someone, especially someone we hold in high regard or care for, can drastically affect our self-esteem. Whether you "lose" or "win," an argument might also affect your self-image.

Charlotte's image as a helpful younger sister who earns her keep in the apartment is at stake. Emma's image as a stern but just older sister who provides for her family without being taken advantage of is at stake. What if the other party has good reasons to think you're not what you present yourself as? Your self-image is really what's at stake for you.

What to Do About It

Understand that this all-or-nothing thinking (I'm helpful or useless, I'm stern or a pushover) is wrong. It doesn't apply here. Build a more complex image of yourself. Sometimes, you'll have to act "out of character." That's okay because you aren't a character in a play but a complex human being.

As you realize this about yourself, understand that the same thing applies to the other person. Hold firm in who you believe yourself to be, but don't panic if you must let go for a moment.

What If I Don't Want to Argue?

The first question that needs to be answered as a potential argument rears its head is *whether it's even worth it to engage*. Indeed, you don't have to waste energy on every disagreement, but being non-confrontational and a people-pleaser to the extreme is incredibly unhealthy.

If someone or something is bothering you, and you keep arguing with yourself about whether to bring it up, you probably should. You keep going back and forth because, deep down, you know that standing down means you'll get taken for granted. Your feelings of insecurity will be left to fester, and the person you're mad at doesn't even have the chance to fix anything.

On the other hand, if you engage in an existing argument or start a new one, it may exacerbate the problem. The other party may get even more upset, and both of your feelings could get hurt despite anyone's intentions. It could even cause irreparable damage to the relationship between the two of you.

Engaging in an argument shouldn't be this nerve-wracking. Confrontation is always going to be challenging, and uncomfortable feelings will always be involved, but you can't expect to get better at it with no practice. When there's an issue, speak up. It's not worth keeping the peace with short-term tactics for a crumbling relationship anyway.

What's Really Holding You Back?

Not confronting a problem doesn't make it go away, so there are other things that make us default to non-confrontation. Confronting someone is dangerous, so we've withheld permission to argue from ourselves. Silence is safe, except not really. Analyze what you're saying to yourself when you assert that arguing is always bad.

I Don't Like Arguing

Most people don't. But you must argue if respect is being taken away from you, you're being ignored, or your voice is actively stifled. You have to take a stand because it's a healthy thing to do.

I'm Scared of Alienating Those I Argue With

Fear is a supremely useful emotion. It means that you're looking out for yourself and your loved ones. It's very unlikely that you'll alienate your loved ones with one argument, and much more likely that you already are by not giving them a chance to do right by you. Embrace your fear, and face it.

I'm Not Good at Making My Point

You argue from your own authority, and that's enough. As much as an argument feels like a battle zone, it's not. So why feel the need to make your point perfectly? You also won't get any good without practice, so make your point and be satisfied with it.

Arguments Are All about Winning, Which I Don't Like

"Winning" an argument can look different for everyone, though it usually means getting what you want. At the end of the day, we use arguments to enact a change, and winning an argument means the change we want will take place. At the end of a productive argument, your perception of "winning" may have changed to a "win" being meeting the other person in the middle.

How Can I Argue with Someone Who Has Power over Me?

The first thing to understand about power is that it's imaginary. Someone's power over you is whatever you imagine that power to be. This is just one more mental obstacle you're imposing on yourself.

You may think like this when you have to confront your boss or parent about something, but every boss needs workers, and every parent needs children to be who they are. All power originates from within us.

When I'm Honest and Truthful, I'm Not Taken Seriously

Being honest and showing your true feelings always builds your credibility. As previously mentioned, feelings are the crux of all arguments. Hiding your true feelings means you're actively working against yourself. If you're honest about your feelings, maybe you're not believed because of some other mistake you've made subconsciously.

In My Experience, Telling the Truth Is Dangerous

This isn't an axiom that's applicable to every argument. If you feel this way, it's more indicative of your relationships than a universal truth. Telling the truth shouldn't be dangerous. Analyze if you truly are in any real danger for telling the truth or if you're making that judgment due to having been burned in the past.

We Always Yell, and Nobody Wins in the End

There's usually very little listening if there's a lot of yelling. If you begin to listen, you're already starting to win. There are always other vulnerable emotions hidden just under anger or judgment. What pain drives this argument? Listen, and ask questions. The time for you to tell your side of the story is not when insults are being hurled at you.

What If I'm up against a Wall of Prejudice?

Although we all have prejudices, certain preconceived notions may be set in stone for some people. As you realize this, you feel as if you're arguing with a brick wall. If you feel as if nothing you're saying is getting through, your "win" may just be taking this experience with you and retreating.

Prejudice is built by self-interest, and reasoning doesn't work against self-interest. What may work is having the other person believe that you, too, are arguing in their best interest. Otherwise, be aware of someone's prejudices, and make a tactical retreat. If reason trumped all, we wouldn't have any prejudices in the first place.

How Do I Even Begin to Formulate an Argument?

You don't have to take out a pen and paper to formulate an argument. When an argument is in progress, that's out of the question anyway. If you're at a loss for words, try to structure your argument like a story.

Humans are predisposed to listen to stories. In fact, world memory champions are able to remember an astounding number of unrelated sequences and facts just by constructing stories around them. As people, we really like stories, so structure your argument like one.

If you want to bring attention to the consequences, start from the end. Otherwise, it's never a bad idea to start a story from the beginning.

When to Throw in the Towel? What We Can and Can't Change

Trying to engage in every argument is both emotionally and mentally exhausting. As you encounter more and more arguments, you'll realize that some of them are difficult beyond their rewards. The other person may be purposefully acting to annoy or get a rise out of us, their prejudices are too much to deal with, or they're completely unwilling to display their true feelings for you to see.

You can control your own reaction to this information, but you can't control anything the other party says or does. Where you draw your own boundaries depends on what you're comfortable with. In the beginning, this may be earlier than you'd like. Be realistic. Some discomfort is to be expected, but short-term solutions are okay to use for arguments that don't seem to have an end.

In a healthy argument, you're both on the same team. Listen, share your feelings, and always stay curious about what the other person is experiencing from their point of view.

Chapter 10: 23 Strategies to End a Conversation Smoothly

Conversations can happen anywhere—at an event, at a shop, while driving, on the phone, over a video call, etc. Along with starting a conversation, it's crucial to always have a strong exit plan which doesn't leave the impression that you're in a hurry, can't be bothered anymore, or are just disinterested. Ending a conversation is as crucial as starting one.

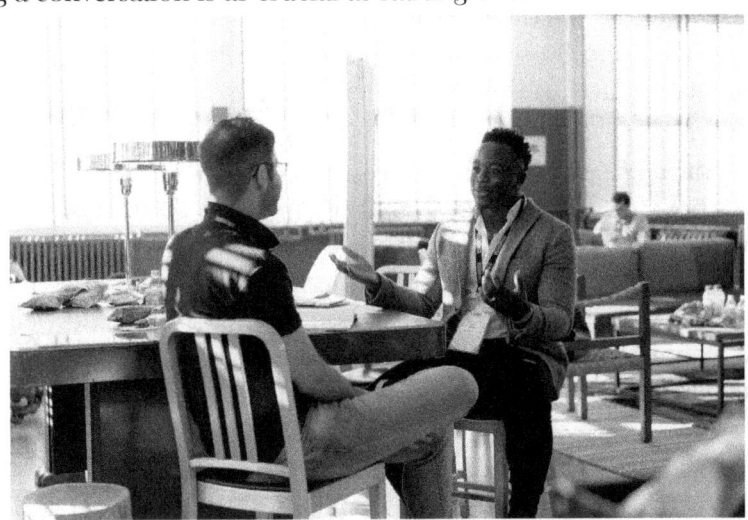

Conversations can happen anywhere—at an event, at a shop, while driving, or on the phone.
https://www.pexels.com/photo/photo-of-men-having-conversation-935949/

When you start a conversation positively and end it abruptly, you could undo all of your previous work and put the other person in a negative mood. Try to end conversations well to leave a positive impression and increase your chances of speaking with the person again. Each conversation you have will end differently, so familiarize yourself with all of your options beforehand.

Make a lasting impression people will remember when you end a conversation and make a good first impression. Sometimes conversations can become awkward, so knowing how to leave a situation is a useful skill to have. You should gracefully end it as soon as you've determined whether the conversation has reached its elastic limit.

When you realize you're bored, it's better to stop talking. Sometimes, you end up saying things that are out of place or start repeating yourself when you run out of things to say. When an interaction reaches its peak and starts to wane, leave to end it professionally. This will make people want more of your time as a result. Instead of waiting for things to get awkward, you should end it with a sense of excitement.

What Causes an Awkward End to a Conversation?

When a conversation slows down to the point where each person is only speaking once every 30 seconds, it is likely coming to an end. It doesn't feel right when it gets to the point where there is nothing else to say, and one of you physically separates from the other out of boredom.

It's a warning sign that the conversation won't go well when you're unsure of how to end it but are frantically trying to think of something to say until someone else steps in. Making a big impact right away and then waiting until the energy is almost gone is not a good way to end a conversation. Whether or not it started out well, it should end well. Being glad that a conversation has ended indicates it did not go well. When there is no excitement – and there is also bad body language – conversations are difficult.

How to End a Conversation on a Good Note

If you had a positive impact on the other person during your interaction, make an effort to keep the momentum by making a strong exit. You have one more chance to affect how the conversation feels at its end. You did well if the interactions produced only positive feelings. Have a plan for how you want the conversation to end, such as "It was nice talking to you, hope to see you again," or "I'm glad we met, or "I'm looking forward to more meetings like this, but now I need to take care of something." Without a solid exit strategy, it would be impossible to leave a positive impression.

Conversation-Ending Strategies for Various Situations

In casual or cooperative conversations, consider the following options for exiting, which will make the other person remember you positively. Whether you're talking to a friend or an acquaintance, at a social gathering such as a party, or to a stranger on the road, you can use any of these options to end your conversation.

1. Ask about Their Plans for the Future

Talk about a future plan, like an occasion that was mentioned during your conversation with them. Ask them if they plan to do anything over the weekend. This implies you should direct the conversation's final topics in the direction you want them to go. They will be open to your closing remarks because discussing their future plans puts them in a positive frame of mind. "Do have a great time with the XYZ plans" is a good note to end the discussion. You will have succeeded in getting them to feel you are concerned about their future plans and to talk about it after the conversation.

2. Propose Meeting up with Them Later

Offer to spend time with them later. When you're talking to a friend or coworker, you can ask if they'd like to go for lunch with you, and if they agree, you've successfully created an avenue to share mutual interests. You can end the conversation by saying, "I'd like to continue this conversation during our lunch." They will happily walk away anticipating lunch and feeling good about your conversation with them.

3. Look Uninterested

If you are the listener and want to end a conversation, look into the distance rather than directly at the speaker. Most speakers expect you to look at them from time to time to demonstrate your interest in what they are saying, and if you look away for too long, they will likely get the message. Sometimes it's hard to express your disinterest in a conversation, and you have to rely on passing an indirect message and hoping the speaker gets the hint.

4. Make a Departure Hint

At the climax of the conversation, as you notice energy dwindling, prepare their minds to expect an end at any moment by saying, "One last thing before I leave." Because you informed them beforehand, they won't have the impression that you are being rude. Even if you carry on talking for a while, they are already aware of your intention to end the conversation sometime soon.

5. Pretend You're Checking in with the Host

If you initiate a conversation with someone at an event, you can use checking in on the host as an exit tactic. If the event is big, you will be seen as popular. Finish your conversation with, "I realize I didn't greet the host. I should leave now. It was a pleasure speaking with you." You can use this on friends or strangers to escape an awkward situation and get some fresh air.

6. Point Your Toes to the Exit

This strategy works if the speaker notices the hint. Your toes pointing toward an exit indicate you want to leave, and hopefully, the speaker picks up on your cue. This strategy has a low impact because not everyone will understand the message you want to convey, and others will ignore it in a bid to continue boring you by continuing to talk.

7. Distance Yourself

Maintain distance from the speaker, but gradually and step by step. The speaker will soon realize you want to be somewhere else and will dismiss you. If they keep talking, keep putting distance between you until it becomes difficult for them to communicate with you. This is a subtle way of saying you want to leave without actually saying so.

8. Finish with a Summary of Their Story

During the conversation, pay attention to the other person's great/awkward/awesome/funny memorable story and recall it when you want to end the conversation. This will rekindle their emotions as you express your gratitude for sharing. Finish the conversation by saying, "I'm so glad we met. I appreciate you sharing this lovely story; I could identify with it. It's been fantastic!" Remembering a story tells them you were paying attention, and they won't feel awkward when you close the conversation.

9. Take Advantage of Your WristWatch

Keep looking at your watch to convey the message that you are in a hurry. A non-verbal signal can easily be ignored by a stubborn speaker, but you can make it clearer by mentioning the time. The conversation could end with something like, "Wow, the time has really flown by, and I never noticed. It's already getting late. It was a pleasure to meet you." You can now walk away without feeling uncomfortable.

10. Set a Time Limit

A subtler version of checking your watch is to inform them you will be leaving in a few minutes. This is similar to setting a time limit for the conversation to keep all parties informed. By saying, "I should go in a few minutes, even though I would have loved to hear more stories," you have told them your time is limited and you need to end the conversation.

11. Excuse Yourself

Saying "Excuse me, please" will end a conversation." You don't have to explain why you need to be excused. You either need to speak to someone else or go somewhere. In any case, excusing yourself has made clear your wish to depart.

12. Take Advantage of Your Family or Friend

Pointing to a friend or acquaintance will also effectively end the conversation. The other person may feel less important or interesting as a result, but you are under no obligation to explain. Say, "Oh, there's my friend. Although I enjoyed our conversation, I must go and see him/her".

13. Send Your Regards to a Mutual Friend

Is your conversation with a friend? If you have mentioned a relative, friend, or acquaintance during your conversation, you can use this to draw a conclusion. Simply tell them to give your regards to the person, saying, "I have to go but don't forget to tell our friend I said hello!"

14. Excuse Them

If you met the person while they were doing something and interrupted them with a conversation, end the conversation by excusing yourself and allowing them to continue their chores. Say something like, "It was great talking with you. I should leave you to finish your chores now."

15. Use Handshake

Surprisingly, handshakes are also used to end conversations. You can start and end a conversation with a handshake, but you must wait for it to be accepted. Consider asking someone for directions and, when they've finished, offer a handshake and thank them. Although it depends on the situation and the individuals involved, this is a professional way to end a conversation.

16. Look around for Inspiration

Look around your surroundings for a cue to help you exit a conversation. It could be the food you're eating reminding you of dinner to be made at home, or it could be an approaching train you must board. You can say, "That's the next train. I shouldn't miss this one to avoid getting home late." Look around you for whatever the cue.

17. Take a Seat or Take a Walk

If you have the conversation standing, ask to be seated as a way to end it. If you've been sitting for a while, you can also ask to stand or go for a walk. The idea is to use the opposite of what you're doing as an excuse to end the conversation. End the conversation with "Wow! We've been standing for a long time. I'll go take a seat now. I thoroughly enjoyed our conversation!" In situations like this, relief is understandable.

18. Use Home as an Exit Strategy

You can use the desire to return home as an exit strategy. Any justification for your hasty return should be relatable and plausible. It could be to assist your partner, to help your parent make a stop at the stores, or to arrive home early before your loved ones become concerned. The conversation is concluded with, "Is it already that late? I need to get going before my parents become concerned!" Don't lie because you may run into your conversation partner again if you don't get home on time.

19. Make a Phone Call

Phone calls can come to your rescue when you need to end a conversation smoothly. You can call a friend, family or colleague. You should conclude your conversation by saying, "I would have loved to continue chatting, but I need to call someone right now. Hope we can talk later?"

20. Exchange Contact Information

Is it a networking event for professionals? Then you should have already exchanged contact information, which you can use to end the conversation, as you say: "It was a pleasure speaking to you. I will send you an email." This generates a lot of hope, expectation, and excitement.

21. Thank Them

"Thank you" is a simple way to end a conversation without ruining the mood. Make direct eye contact while saying it with sincerity. Remember, they can see your emotions through your eyes, so be genuine in your appreciation. Conclude the conversation with "Thank you for chatting; I should be leaving now. Goodbye."

22. Use Gestures at the Workplace

In the workplace, gestures can be used to end conversations rather than actual words. You can walk up to the exit door and hold the handle to signal your wish to leave. Alternatively, walk with the person toward their office or desk rather than offering them a seat in yours. Ask if you can meet them later because you have unfinished business to attend to first. Offer to continue the conversation after lunch, or you can kindly remind them of their unfinished work and send them on their way. In a fast-paced setting like the working world, it's easy to pick up on cues and end conversations without feeling awkward or stressed.

23. Tell Them Your Battery Is Running Low

If you're on a call or video call, you can end it quickly by saying your battery is low, you need to switch to another call, or the connection is bad, so you'll call back later. Tell them you can't talk while driving and promise you'll call back. Always say you will call them back later when you want to end a video or phone call abruptly. Once the call's agenda is finished, say goodbye and thank the other party.

When you end conversations well, you can leave a lasting memory and make amazing friendships no matter where you are or who you are talking to. If your exit strategy complements your chat partner and makes the person feel memorable and liked, you have made a grand exit. One single exit strategy to achieve this during a conversation is "It has been so wonderful speaking to you. I will certainly remember you." This type of conversation ender will warm the heart of anyone who hears it.

How to End a Conversation with a Chatterbox

Even when you're not paying attention, this type of person can talk you to death. It seems they would rather speak and have their opinions heard. Don't give a coworker a chance to get comfortable in their chatter. Remind them you have a task to do and will return to the conversation when you have time. It is easier to end conversations with your coworkers if you use gestures to indicate you are busy or if you position yourself close to the door, ready to leave as soon as you can.

If you meet a stranger and they turn out to be a chatterbox, you can fake a phone call to get them to stop talking while also giving you an opportunity to escape. Look away and rarely respond to their conversation. Hopefully, they'll get the message and end the conversation. It can be difficult to end conversations without appearing rude when you're the listener. When all other methods of signaling the chatterbox have failed, you can use the silent treatment. Keep quiet, and they'll stop talking when you don't respond.

How to End a Conversation When Someone Shows Disinterest

As the speaker, you should be able to notice when your chat partner has lost interest in the conversation. One way is to observe their body language. Signs of boredom will include a loss of focus, eye contact, and distraction, which is a clear sign that it's time to end the conversation.

In situations like this, use some of the following methods to end the conversation without losing any dignity.

- Appreciate them for their time and say goodbye. Keep it simple and straightforward.
- Ask to make use of the restroom. This is also an easy way if you are in a place with a restroom.
- Excuse the person to get back to what they were doing when you met them.
- Quickly make a phone call and excuse yourself. Phone calls have helped many people end conversations, especially boring ones.
- Compliment something about them, maybe their smile or hair, and ask to leave immediately.

Picture yourself enjoying a mouthwatering meal and then getting a terrible dessert. It's not the nice meal, but the awful dessert that will be the first thing you recall. This is comparable to a conversation where the first impression was positive, but the last impression wasn't the same. Poor first impressions can be rescued if you leave a great last impression. If you strike up a conversation, prepare an escape route in advance. Stop talking when people are excited and interested. You'd have a better chance of meeting and speaking to them again if you ended your previous conversation on a positive note.

An all-around exit strategy, regardless of what was discussed or where the conversation is taking place, would be to thank your chat partner for their time and tell them you look forward to seeing them later. You can say things like, "I enjoyed speaking with you. I hope to do it again another time," "It was nice seeing you again, thank you for coming," and "I am grateful our paths crossed."

Conclusion

Improving your communication skills can elevate several aspects of your professional and private life. Effective communication gives us a way to understand events, people, and situations successfully without leaving much room for misinterpretation. Good communicators adapt well to diverse environments and help you get along well with people. They are also able to cultivate mutual respect and trust with everyone around them, as well as create a healthy space for problem-solving and generating innovative ideas.

It is widely believed that employees' productivity can be improved by encouraging good organization-wide communications. Many people think that interacting with others is easy, especially those who have never interacted with someone from a different background or hold significantly different opinions and beliefs. There is always a chance of disconnection in mutual understanding, which could reach the point of boiling anger and conflict. However, working on your communication skills teaches you how to communicate your point of view and process that of others while keeping your head and emotions in check.

Being an excellent communicator will always make you valuable. However, it has become a particularly crucial skill in today's modern age. We consume a large amount of information while talking to people, scrolling through social media, shopping, watching TV, or running errands every single day. Having good communication skills allows us to feel less overwhelmed because it helps us decode the messages being delivered to us. Communication is not just about sharing and sending information. It also has a lot to do with how we receive, process, and react to it, and it enables us to gain insight into the emotions behind the messages we receive.

Strong communication enriches our personal and professional relationships. It makes us better decision-makers and encourages us to compromise in difficult situations. Being able to express ourselves and speak our minds with ease can boost our confidence and make us more assertive.

The best communicators are often the first ones to come up with great solutions. They are advocates and initiators of change, inspiring and motivating those around them. This is why a lack of communication skills can be a deal breaker in the work environment. It can also put relationships on the line.

While some people are talented, eloquent speakers, others require more practice to get their messages through to an audience. While it takes a lot of time and effort, anyone can become an excellent communicator if they put their mind to it. Now that you have read this book, you know how to strike up conversations, actively listen to people, improve your social intelligence, master the art of storytelling and improve your public speaking. This book is the key to improved communication skills and effective interactions. Applying the knowledge provided in this guide can help you avoid misinterpretations and improve all your relationships. The better your communication skills, the higher the levels of mutual trust and respect you will gain in your interactions.

Part 2: How to Analyze People

Decoding Human Behavior and Body Language So You Can Read People like a Book Effortlessly

Introduction

So, you want to analyze people like a pro. Well, you've made the right decision. The world we live in today has become increasingly sophisticated, meaning it's tough to keep up with people and whether or not they're being honest with you. You don't want to be the one person in the room who's always out of the loop, unaware of what's really going on because you missed a cue. So, choosing to master the language of what's not being said is indeed a smart call.

Another smart decision you've taken is choosing this book in particular. This book will focus on how you can figure out what makes people tick – and by showing you how it's almost impossible to lie in body language. It will also show you essential tips on studying human behavior and offer very practical tips and methods to determine someone's intentions or true thoughts. You can rest assured that everything you learn in this book is backed by scientific research. You can bank on the information here to give you great results.

Learning to read people is an important skill that everyone should take the time to learn. Sure, it's easy to assume that only those in fields like sociology, criminology, or psychology should bother to understand what drives every human interaction and action, but this couldn't be further from the case. Learning to analyze people could mean the difference between never getting ahead in life and skyrocketing to the heights you've always dreamed of attaining. It could mean improving your personal and professional relationships to allow smoother interactions and more rewarding outcomes for everyone involved. It doesn't matter what field you're in. What cannot be denied is that studying human behavior and body language is priceless and will always be worth the effort.

Unlike other books on the market, this one is written clearly in plain English. This makes your reading experience stress-free by keeping concepts extremely simple to understand. You can bank on there being references to studies that have been carried out on human behavior and their results and implications. This book will serve as a hands-on guide on how you can decode human behavior like a pro and read body language as if it were a book. You'll learn about deception, how to identify it, and how to deal with it using various effective tips and methods. You will also discover what kinds of body language there are and their meanings in various contexts. Whether you're a pro at this or just diving into the world of the human psyche and how it gives itself away through the body, you'll find something worthwhile in this book!

Chapter 1: What Can Human Behavior Tell Us?

You have an unconscious mind that is extremely powerful. This mind is responsible for all sorts of things, like how creative you are, your personality, your values and beliefs, the automatic processes your body runs, your memory, body language, and much more. Science has found that out of all your brain activities, only about 5 percent are conscious. The rest of them are under the purview of the unconscious mind. What does this imply?

When you look at the body language people use, you can learn quite a bit about the thoughts they're having at the moment and what they're feeling. This is why choosing to decipher the meaning behind human behavior will help you decipher why people act the way they do.

What Can Human Behavior Reveal?

When analyzing why people choose to act the way they do, it's easy to simply analyze what they believe and what they value and desire that would drive them to choose their actions. Let's assume, for instance, you notice Pamela leaving the apartment building and heading straight for the grocery store. You might assume that she chose to do this because she would like to pick up items for a healthy dinner she wants to make herself at home. She believes the grocery store is the best place to pick up the ingredients she needs to prepare that meal. However, when working in the context of beliefs and desires, you might find a lot of wiggle room to work with. In other words, if it turns out Pamela is actually a chef, it could be that she's going to the store not because she wants dinner but because it's part of her job description.

It becomes obvious then that trying to work out what drives someone to do what they do requires a foundation much more reliable than the twin pillars of belief and desire. There are different ways to analyze human desire that psychology has come up with. Still, for the most part, there's no congruence in the way they interpret things, which leaves us with all kinds of motivations for why people act one way and not another. For instance, those who follow the Skinnerian method believe that it isn't helpful to think in terms of desires and beliefs but to take a scientific stance when looking at the environmental impact of constant behaviors. Other psychologists take a more cognitive approach by considering motivation through the lens of information and its implications to explain the motive. For those taking a Freudian approach, it's all about the subconscious, as this is the driving force behind what makes us act the way we do. For this group of psychologists, our conscious minds don't factor into the equation all that much.

James Madison University professor of psychology, Gregg Henriques, has developed a more integrated form of language that can help us piece together the factors that drive human behavior. He was inspired by the critical points discovered by those across various schools of thought, from cognitive psychology to psychodynamic theory, among other viewpoints. He puts them together in a way that allows more cohesion when breaking down human motivation and behavior. He has concluded that we can use three major processes to understand human drive. They are:

- Investment
- Social influence
- Justification

Altogether, these three form what he has called the unified framework. Let's take a look at each one in detail.

Investment: This is the amount of effort you put into something to create the change you seek. So, let's assume you're Pamela. You may go to the grocery store because you want to make yourself some dinner, or you may be going there only because it's part of your job description as a chef. The act of heading to the store is the investment in this case. Investment here refers to everything that goes into making the action you take possible, including figuring out the best time to leave for the store, which route to take, making a list, figuring out how much money to spend, assessing how long the task will take, the risks of going to the store versus not going, and so on.

These are all considered with the end goal of attaining a fixed result. The result could be that Pamela gets to enjoy a delicious dinner or that she gets to prepare a great meal for the patrons of the restaurant she works at. When you look at it this way, it's natural to question what it is that primes her to make these investments. The fact is that there are certain things we're all driven by, including the need for food, sustenance, protection, status, safety, and more.

You also have to factor in the fact that we all have different emotional set points, and a bulk of these are affected by our genetics. For instance, if you're an extrovert, you'll naturally seek to recharge by connecting with others. For an introvert, recharging is a matter of withdrawing from other people. There's also the effect of everything you've experienced in your life, which will affect how much you invest in a given course of action. Suppose Pamela has experienced being starved or not having any money to take care of herself. In that case, it stands to reason that she will be driven to head to the store to shop.

Social Influence: Humans are naturally social, meaning we cannot consider our personal experiences without comparing them to others. It's not normal for us to be driven to do things without influence from the surrounding society. So, when we talk about social influence, we have to think of it in several ways. For one, we must consider how it is that one person's choices might have some effect on another person's investment. For instance, did Pamela want to go willingly to the store, or is she only going because someone else who should have gone in her place decided not to at the last minute? Did she just find out that a key ingredient is finally available in the store, so she had to get it before it ran out again? According to Henriques, you must consider cooperation and competition regarding social influence. Equally important is whether the actions taken will drive the people to rely on each other more or make them less dependent on each other.

The other light in which we must consider social influence is through the lens of it being a resource, which refers to how it's able to get other people to act in ways that align with the results we seek. In other words, it comes down to how people rate us in terms of the amount of respect they deem us worthy of and how valuable they consider us to be. This is demonstrated in how much they choose to invest in how well we're doing by listening, showing up when we need them, and sacrificing things that matter to them for our sake. Consider Pamela once more; if her boss asked her to go to the store, that immediately shows you that he has some social influence over her. But if she weren't invested in her job and chose to disregard his request that she go shopping, we can assume that he has no social influence over her. Suppose she's going to the store because her partner at home decided they weren't interested in going to the store as they used to in the past. In that case, it could mean that Pamela has lost some social influence over them.

Justification: According to Henriques' unified framework, justification is to be considered in the light of verbal and written communication, specifically regarding what he labels their "systematic structure" and "legitimizing function." In other words, justification is about the questions you can ask and the answers they lead to surrounding the matter of the reality of a situation versus an ideal or desired situation. For instance, let's assume Pamela has to go to the store because, for whatever reason, her partner has refused. She could justify her going to the store by saying, "I'm more than happy to help you out for a change because you deserve a break," or she could say, "I'm not going to bed tonight without eating something for dinner." These are both valid reasons. Or let's assume Pamela is going to the store because her boss asked. It could be that her justification is, "It's part of the job, so I'm going to do it." Justifications are the reasons you have for doing things — as well as reasons for choosing not to. It encompasses such matters as scientific claims, societal laws, and personal rationalizations.

Studying human behavior to understand its motivations will reveal a lot when it comes to the three prongs of investment, social influence, and justification. So, you should always remember that every action and inaction is, above all things, a form of investment. The reason we do anything at all is that - one way or another - we have weighed the risk of not choosing one course of action versus another, especially in light of the results we'd rather have. Once you have this in mind, you can then turn your attention to the matter of societal influence to see how the investments we choose to make or ignore can affect others and how they, in turn, help us come to a conclusion about whether or not an investment is worth it. Then, you turn your attention to the explanations offered by one and all to justify the choices made.

Studies on Human Behaviors and Their Meanings in Set Situations

When it comes to human behavior, you should note that it covers everything from verbal and non-verbal communication to language. Having said that, it is important to note that there's no straightforward answer about what particular behaviors actually mean, so when attempting to interpret one, you cannot consider it in isolation. You also have to consider the context in which the behavior is being displayed. With that out of the way, let's look at some studies on what a certain behavior might mean in a fixed setting. By *setting*, we refer to things like context, environment, culture, etc.

According to research by Matsumoto, Hwang, Skinner, and Frank, it has been found that when people lie, they are often more likely to act in ways that do not support their words or the context of what they're saying than those who are telling the truth. For instance, if Sam stole something from the mall, and he chooses to claim he didn't, he might nod his head while lying, giving himself away through what is known as leakage, which can happen both verbally and non-verbally. However, it's important to note that the issue here isn't the fact that he's nodding his head. That - in and of itself - is not enough to know if he's being honest or dishonest. It's more about whether he remains consistent with his statements or at least the context in which he passes along his message.

Human behavior can serve to regulate the way others communicate with us. For instance, when a law enforcement officer wants to regulate the actions of a suspect or the way they communicate, they could touch the suspect's arm to show they'd like to speak next or that they're about to interrupt them. This is indicated by Knapp and Hall in their book, "Nonverbal Communication in Human Interaction."

Cultural differences affect people's eye contact.
https://www.pexels.com/photo/woman-wearing-teal-dress-sitting-on-chair-talking-to-man-2422280/

Eye contact comes down to the culture of the people involved in an interaction. For instance, in the United States, establishing eye contact with someone who's asking questions implies a level of honesty. It could also imply encouragement. When eye contact is avoided, it could be because the speaker isn't being honest or they're not comfortable with the matter being discussed (according to Ikeda and Tidwell in "The Providers Guide to Quality and Culture: Nonverbal Communication, Vermont Department of Health.")

Yet another interesting human behavior is the amount of space one puts between themselves and others. No matter who you are or where you go, you have personal space around you. This is your territory. It has been found that you can demonstrate the amount of social distance between people by noting the physical distance between them. This principle of distance is known as proxemics, as espoused by cultural anthropologist Edward T. Hall. In the next chapter, we'll take a critical look at the history of the science of analyzing human behavior, so you can have a clear picture of where it all started and how far it has come.

Chapter 2: The History of Human Behavior Analysis

People have always found ways to communicate with each other, even before we came up with our complex language systems. The same applies to all other living beings on the face of the earth. We communicate using facial expressions, body posture, touch, intonation, eye movement, and space. All of these are important when passing along messages, but for the most part, they're all unconscious. This necessitates the analysis of human behavior. In this chapter, we're going to look at the history of human behavior analysis, also known as behaviorism.

A History of Human Behavior Analysis

This field of study arose out of a need to understand the actions of living beings. It is based on the assumption that the way we act is either reflexive as a result of some form of stimulus around us or on account of the consequences to be dealt with, including ones that will cement the likelihood of certain choices being made in the future in the form of rewards and punishment. Along with this is how motivated you are to behave a certain way and the presence or absence of a certain stimulus. While those who study behavior know that heredity has a role to play, they turn their attention to what's happening in the environment.

Pavlov and His Dogs

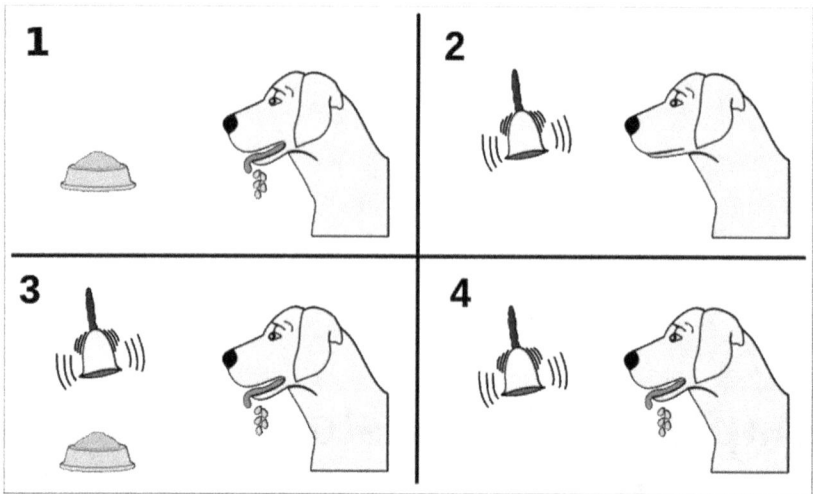

Pavlov used dogs to come up with classical conditioning.
Maxxl², CC BY-SA 4.0 <https://creativecommons.org/licenses/by-sa/4.0>, via Wikimedia Commons: https://commons.wikimedia.org/wiki/File:Pavlov%27s_dog_conditioning.svg

We can trace the history of human behavior analysis from Pavlov's time. In 1897, Russian psychologist Ivan Pavlov was responsible for coming up with the process we all know today as classical conditioning. This process involves taking stimuli that used to be neutral and connecting them with other stimuli to cause the desired behavior. The most famous of Pavlov's work involved what he did with dogs back in 1897. This critical experiment is what gave birth to behaviorism as we know it. Pavlov measured how much his dogs salivated by putting a tube in their mouths. When the dogs would smell or see food, they would naturally salivate. Then, the researcher chose to ring a bell each time the dogs were offered food. He started to notice that they had learned to associate the sound of the bell with the arrival of food. So, he began ringing the bell without offering them food, and despite that, the dogs still salivated at the sound.

Thorndike and His Cats

Yet another important figure to consider is Edward Thorndike. He was an American psychologist who wanted to understand what it took to learn new things. He published The Law of Effect in 1905, stating that whenever you have a stimulus and its attached response, you're going to find that the connection between the two is what leads one to act in a specific manner. In other words, we act the way we do at every point in time because we want the best outcome for the circumstance in which we find ourselves. For this reason, we'll keep doing something over and over if we get rewards by taking that course of action.

Thorndike proved the integrity of his theory by working with cats, putting them in a puzzle box equipped with a lever. Whenever a cat could correctly work the lever, it would open up the trap door and make its way out of the box. The cat bothered to learn how to work the lever because it wanted to get out. This was its motivation. Thorndike proved that if you want to change behavior, you could change the outcome and/or change what you deem desirable. You can find all the things he discovered in "Animal Intelligence," which he published in 1911.

Watson and Little Albert

Another critical time in the history of behavior analysis is 1913, with the publication of the book "Psychology as the Behaviorist Views" by John B. Watson. In that book, Watson introduced the concept of "behaviorism." This was new psychology based on the objective study of observable behavior. Watson's behaviorism grew out of his rejection of the psychoanalytic theory of Sigmund Freud. Instead, Watson argued for a science distinct from what he referred to as the "old psychology," which he characterized as unscientific because it relied too heavily on subjective introspection, was unreliable, and lacked objective evidence.

Watson is the father of behaviorism. He once said that given 12 healthy infants, he could place them in a controlled world, pick any of them, and train them to become whoever he wanted them to be, so they could become specialists at anything with the skills he chose them, professional or criminal. He claimed he could do that regardless of the children's ancestry, abilities, tendencies, talents, and anything else that might be considered a hindrance.

Watson proved his theories by carrying out the famous Little Albert experiment of 1920. He had worked with the founding principles of classical conditioning, proving it with an infant who was only 9 months old. He first offered this child some objects: soft items, furry items, a white rat, and flames. At the start of the study, all the items were considered neutral, and Albert, the infant, didn't react dramatically to them. Later on, when Watson would offer Little Albert the white rat, he would accompany the creature with a loud sound. This caused the poor child to grow rather frightened of the creature, even when the sound was no longer accompanying it. The child also became frightened of all things furry. While this was a very inhumane experiment, Watson did show that, for the most part, human behavior isn't hardwired into us all from birth one hundred percent of the time. Instead, it is something we learn. He demonstrated that neutral stimuli could become conditioned stimuli through the mechanisms of learning and experience.

Skinner and His Box

Burrhus Frederic Skinner (1904-1990) was an American psychologist, behaviorist, author, inventor, and social philosopher. He was the Edgar Pierce Professor of Psychology at Harvard University from 1958 until his retirement in 1974. Skinner considered free will an illusion, and human action depends on the consequences of previous actions. The "behavior" (action, speech) is repeated if the consequences are good. If the consequences are not good, it is not repeated. This is reinforcement that is taken to its limit when delivered in a very swift and specific manner. How did he do this?

In 1929, Skinner got into Harvard to study psychology, and three years later, he came up with an operant conditioning chamber. He called it the "Skinner box." He would place a small creature in the box, and to be rewarded, the creature would have to work a lever or push a button. In this experiment, he demonstrated that the behavior of jumping when a button is pushed was reinforced. This was called instrumental conditioning. However, after many sessions with his newly formed theory of operant psychology, Skinner began using these results to demonstrate instead that behavior could be shaped through reinforcement, using positive and negative events to either increase or decrease a given action. Skinner's research contributed significantly to the development of applied behavior analysis, which uses principles and methods derived from the operant conditioning paradigm to improve socially significant behaviors such as those related to autism and alcoholism.

Skinner's experimental research on operant conditioning had its philosophical basis in George Santayana's dictum: "Those who do not learn from history are doomed to repeat it." Although human behavior is based on various conditions (genetic, biochemical, physiological, environmental), behavior only counts for conditioning if it can be repeated. By this criterion, many human behaviors do not qualify as proper subjects for scientific study. For example, social behaviors, such as greeting and all manners of politeness, cannot be observed in a laboratory. They are learned and, therefore, not controlled by the natural environment. Scientific studies cannot define those behaviors that are not operant.

Skinner's radical behaviorism was an extreme form of behaviorism. He believed that it provided a complete picture of human behavior and that any remaining phenomena could be understood as epiphenomena (another way of saying "side effects"). Skinner offered little in the way of explanations for these epiphenomena. However, he also did not deny their existence. Instead, he suggested that they should be seen as more clearly explained on a level he called "operant conditioning."

In 1917, Jacob Robert Kantor received his Ph.D. and was responsible for developing inter-behaviorism. He and other researchers developed the "long-term" conditioning of dogs by forcing them to pee in response to a stimulus, later called "operant conditioning." Skinner initially did not accept this research, as he was not convinced that animals retain all the memories of the experience. After Kantor and others demonstrated their important findings, Skinner began collaborating with Jacob Robert Kantor. By 1924, he had published his book "Principles of Psychology."

In his 1938 book "The Behavior of Organisms," Skinner defined operant behavior as "An operant is a class of responses made by an organism, the probable future responses of which are influenced by their consequences in such a way that these consequences become more and more likely."

Keller's Reinforcement Schedule

In 1938, Fred Keller became part of the faculty at Columbia University. Then, later on, he and Nat Schoenfeld published a paper in Psychological Review suggesting that roughly 80% of human behavior could be explained by the operation of "reinforcement schedules," which they described as "an actual mathematical principle." In their experiments, rats were trained to press one button to get food pellets. The "reinforcement schedule" was based on the ratio of the length of time the rat pressed before getting a pellet compared with the time long after it received a pellet. Skinner read this paper while attending Harvard Summer School and was so moved that he eventually sent Schoenfeld an autographed copy with a note. In the same year, Skinner published his renowned "Behavior of Organisms."

Ray Birdwhistell

A critical part of the history of behaviorism is an anthropologist named Ray Birdwhistell, who established kinesics as a study in 1952. Kinesics studies body language, specifically how humans use gestures and posture to communicate with animals. Birdwhistell published several books, one of them being "Introduction to Kinesics" (1952). According to him, the verbal aspects of our conversation are only responsible for about 30 to 35 percent of the messages we pass along to others. He left an indelible mark on the study of language and how we socially connect with one another using nonverbal cues. According to him, the way we move our bodies comes down to culture and should not be considered universal. His best-known book was "Kinesics and Context."

Birdwhistell was also known for his film, "Micro-cultural Incidents in Ten Zoos. This film shows how different family members from different cultures connect with each other. This film was about the social gaze. A hidden camera was set up to observe people who were checking out animals in various zoos across seven countries, and it showed not just the interactions between family members, but between humans and animals, especially in terms of nonverbal communication.

Research on Facial Expressions

Other aspects of nonverbal communication include social cues, proxemics (distance), chronemics (time), haptics (touch), eye contact, facial expressions, pupil dilation, and how frequently glances occur, oculesics (blink rate), and so on. This study of nonverbal communication began in 1872 when Charles Darwin published "The Expression of the Emotions in Man and Animals." He noted that expressions and gestures are essential aspects of communication and that these tools allow emotions to be conveyed from one being to another.

He sought to answer the questions about why emotions are conveyed in a specific manner, such as a wrinkled nose when one is disgusted or bared teeth when angered. The way he saw it, they had to do with habits that we had used during the earlier part of our evolution. For instance, before you bite someone, you must show your teeth. If you smell something foul, it's natural to wrinkle your nose. So, Darwin posited that facial expressions are simply the result of one's inner state of mind. His theory led to all the research that has been carried out so far on nonverbal communication.

A 2020 study by Bailenson shows that people who can see facial cues projected on avatars that resemble their partners will be much better at gauging what's happening with others on the inside when figuring out other people's personalities.

Other Critical Events in the History of Behavior Analysis

From the 1920s to the 1950s, behaviorism took major prominence in psychology. It would also become relevant in games, poker, and law enforcement. At this time, the researchers were desperate for theories they could work with empirically and contribute to understanding human motivations.

1943 is the year we discovered the idea of *shaping* in behaviorism. Shaping is about reinforcing behaviors that are more like those you'd like someone to exhibit. These reinforcements are called successive approximations. In 1944, William Estes and Skinner gave us a monograph that addressed the subject of punishment. With this monograph, they introduced a new term called deprivation. Deprivation is defined as the removal of reinforcement after the behavior has been reinforced. This has a negative effect because it would then prevent the cycle, and the behavior will not happen again. Estes and Skinner gave many examples of how punishment works. By 1945, Skinner put out a powerful paper that addressed the operational analysis of psychological terms. By 1947, he gave a series of lectures on verbal behavior at Harvard.

It is important to note that various kinds of behavior analysis exist, i.e., methodological behaviorism and radical behaviorism.

Modern-Day Fascination with Behavior Analysis

Many people know that the best way to understand and treat an array of problems is to understand the underlying factors that impact them. But what many don't realize is that this idea is not new. In fact, behavior analysis has been around for over 100 years. In recent years, it's faced a bit of a renaissance due to its practical applications for treating chronic illnesses and other challenges faced by society.

But if you read popular articles on this field, you would think behavior analysis was just newly invented. In reality, it has been around ever since psychologists like John B. Watson first used it to try to treat mental illnesses such as addiction and post-traumatic stress disorder in the early 1900s.

Things have changed a lot since the first use of behavior analysis. The field has evolved tremendously in recent years –

, and now behaviors are being studied in ways that weren't possible 100 years ago. Today, behavior analysis is used to help people with everything from chronic illnesses to ADHD. It also treats people with brain injuries, low self-esteem, and other disorders. This renewed interest is based on the idea that understanding what motivates people's behaviors can help treat these problems when all else fails. This may sound intuitive, but it hasn't always been this way.

Behavior analysis is also incredibly important in the legal system and serves as the foundation for everything from child custody to mental health evaluations. It has also been used in courtrooms and legal proceedings and has even helped exonerate people who have been falsely accused of crimes.

Behavior analysts are often called on in the courtroom to make a thorough case for why someone might have committed a crime. The basis of this argument is usually to show that an underlying psychological factor or disorder could explain otherwise questionable behavior. For example, someone might steal because they have an addiction. In other cases, this type of evidence might be crucial for getting a fair trial or being sentenced fairly (no matter what specific crime took place).

But this is just one small part of what behavior analysts do. They use science to try to understand and solve problems ranging from obesity to healthcare, education, and the environment. This way, they're impacting society more than many people realize.

When it comes to getting ahead in your career, being able to analyze behavior will help you stand out. For example, if you can discuss how someone's actions or reactions are influenced by their emotions, you'll be able to challenge those in power and make a bigger impact on society at large. You'll also be able to better understand the real implications of different behaviors that impact people's lives.

The incredible applications of behavior analysis are not limited to healthcare and the legal system, though, and they range from education to community service projects, even planning a home improvement project or a trip abroad. In other words, this is an incredibly important field with so much potential impact on different aspects of modern life.

Chapter 3: Decoding Someone's Verbal Behavior

Behaviorism is a theoretical framework in psychology that studies human and animal behavior. Behaviorists believe that all behavior can be explained without referring to an individual's mental life, beliefs, or desires. In other words, what motivates an individual is different from what they say or do because the concept of motivation originates with goals in mind. This behavior is seen by others which then leads to the desired action.

Behaviorists believe that humans can study human and animal behavior without first referring to mental life as introspections, a theory based on subjective experience and the analysis of consciousness. They reject the concept of introspection because it is considered to be subjective, unreliable, and not verifiable through scientific means. Behaviorists believe that two types of knowledge are used when observing behavior - verbal reports (what one says) and behavioral records (what one does).

When studying behavior, the psychologist must remember that verbal reports are not the same as actual behavior. The reports consist of "ideal" exemplars of behavior and never represent a person's actual behavior. Although it is essential to understand what the speaker really means by their statements, it is equally important to know why they say what they say. The key to understanding why a person says something is by observing their response over time and taking note of patterns in their responses.

Many forms of communication exist; one of the chief forms we rely on is *verbal communication*. In this chapter, we'll talk about the different factors of verbal communication that you need to be on the lookout for when trying to understand what someone's saying and what they're not saying to you. We will look at the tone of voice, speed of the voice, attitude, and the use of negative or positive words.

Tone of Voice

There's the meaning of words on their own, and then there's the added dimension of meaning when you factor in how those words are said. This is why you'll often hear, "It's not about what you said, but how you said it." There's research to back up the fact that the tone of voice can convey so much more meaning. In fact, the tone of voice alone accounts for 38 percent of the message communicated. It wasn't until recently that scientists came to the clear conclusion that various tones of voice can have effects that are just as varied on how we connect with one another.

The University of Southern California had a group of researchers look into many conversations, numbering in the hundreds. They studied these conversations over the course of two years, working with a specially programmed algorithm. They were very interested in how intense human voices can get, as well as the pitch of each voice, showing that emotions were high. In this study, there were no less than a hundred couples, and you can find the results in the Proceedings of Interspeech journal.

What the researchers found was remarkable. They saw that they could predict whether a couple would do well in their marital lives based on their tone of voice. In fact, this factor was much more accurate at foretelling a happy future with each other than professional counselors. This is noteworthy, especially when you think counselors should already be pretty good at deducing what's going on with a couple from their verbal and nonverbal communication cues. Five years after this study, the researchers checked in with the participants. They saw that their algorithm was correct at least 74 percent of the time about how much better or worse a relationship was likely to have gotten. The main point here is this - your tone of voice matters a lot. It can affect the way you connect with others for better or worse, especially those we're close to.

The words you choose and how you say them to others can affect the way you feel with your partner. In turn, your partner's words and tone have the same effect on you. Knowing this can help you figure out how to bring awareness to your interactions to achieve the best outcomes each time. Yet another study showed that when couples choose to express their appreciation for the other person by using the magic words "please" and "thank you," the odds are that their union would be one full of happiness. Even other nonverbal shows of appreciation, like rubbing a partner's arm or kissing them on the forehead, helped them feel connected to each other, handle the bad times better, and not become part of divorce statistics.

Speed of Voice

The speed of your voice is also an indicator of how you feel about the words you're speaking. Throughout your life, you've probably noticed that when you're really passionate about something, the words just seem to flow more quickly. Likewise, your voice's pace will likely turn into a rant if you start getting emotional because of something you're saying or thinking about. The same thing happens if someone's trying to calm down from being upset about something.

Speakers will slow down their voices so they can think more clearly and choose their words carefully. This is why it's been repeatedly proven that the slower we talk, the wiser we are perceived to be by others. Also, everyone has a speed they consider to be normal. These speeds are highly variable from person to person. So, unless you want to be perceived as slow and uninteresting, you need to know precisely what your personal speed is to use this to your advantage. If your voice is significantly slower than others (which is likely due to a lack of confidence in yourself or your personality), watch out. You'll likely have a hard time getting anyone's attention, which makes it more likely that they will tune out the words you're saying.

A study titled "Speed of Speech and Persuasion" was carried out in 1976 by Norman Miller and others and was published in the Journal of Personality and Social Psychology. This study sought to analyze the connection between the speed of speech and changes in attitudes. The rate at which the participants would speak was considered in light of how credible they were and the complexity of the information conveyed. The results of this study showed that the speed at which people speak could affect their credibility in the eyes of others; speaking at a rapid pace was found to be good for persuasion. In contrast, speedy talk reduced the listener's ability to process the contextual information being conveyed.

Another study by Guyer and Fabrigar in May 2016 sought to find how vocal speed and intonation worked together to influence attitudes. Those who participated in the study would first be played a recording that moderately supported the idea of working for one's university in exchange for lower tuition fees. The participants had to write down 10 thoughts that came to their minds as they listened and rate how much those thoughts they had were in favor of the topic at hand. In the end, the participants had to check out their attitudes toward the idea. It was discovered that both the intonation and speed at which the recording was delivered would influence how the listeners perceived the speaker's confidence. This, in turn, affected the listeners' cognitive responses regarding their bias. Speech rate can indicate how confident the speaker is, which, in turn, will influence the speaker's attitude.

How else does vocal speed influence the way you perceive a message? It's actually quite simple: when you're speaking more slowly, people perceive your message as being *far more important when you speak faster.* This is because we fill in the blanks in our own heads as we go along. When anyone says a word or sends a message, we start to imagine what they are saying. We observe how they hold their faces, look at us while they talk, and so on. All of this information we give our brains helps solidify the meaning of what we're listening to or reading. When you speak more slowly, it's easier for us to imagine that the message is more important. This is why people who speak slower are often seen as being more intelligent, while someone who speaks faster would be perceived as less intelligent.

Understanding how the speed of your voice can influence how you're perceived is crucial to being better at communicating with others. It's even more important when trying to help others understand what you mean. If your message is only half-understood, then it will likely be hard for them to follow what you're saying and even harder for them to remember what it was that you said in the first place. So, if you want to get attention, make sure the words that come out of your mouth are clear and easy for others to hear. The same goes for how you say it: slow down or speed up as needed.

Attitude

The attitude someone has when they're speaking can affect the way their message is perceived as well. You can tell from the attitude of the speaker what else it is that they're not saying. When the speaker has a pleasant attitude and appears upbeat and lively, you could assume that they're in a great mood and let that factor into how you read them as they speak. Attitude is so important in all aspects of life, and it can be the difference between success and failure in what we do. It's tough to communicate verbally without some attitude seeping in.

A person's attitude affects the way their message is perceived.
https://www.pexels.com/photo/expressive-multiethnic-couple-having-conflict-on-street-6147230/

Attitude also covers your point of view about various things. For instance, when someone very clearly has a strong stance about a particular issue in life, you'll find that the way they speak to you and the words they choose tend to be very black-and-white, leaving no room for nuance on the matter. Let's assume that you're speaking with someone who has a solid opinion on why they would rather vote for the left or the right. Regardless of how valid the points you bring up against their own views may be, you'll notice they find it difficult to hear you out or register your own ideas. This tells you that they have an ingrained point of view that will not budge. It also keeps them from totally and correctly understanding any other points that do not correlate with or support the ones they hold. Knowing this about the person, it's not hard to see how they could be easily manipulated because of the blind spots they have or to tell what you could say or do to push their buttons and get the desired effect from them. That sounds sinister, but that's how much you can infer from one's attitude on any subject matter.

Attitude in speech can also make it hard to correctly pass a message to others. For instance, you may hire someone to work as a sales manager in your office. Your attitude toward them could be that you assume they should be able to handle the job without needing much in the way of training on account of the credentials they've shown you. Since you've assumed and taken this attitude that they're capable on their own, you may not be so thorough when training them on your company's expectations, procedures, and policies. This could lead to them not being as great at their job as they could or should be, causing them to be unproductive, ruining professional relationships in the workplace, and so on.

Choice of Words

When we speak, the words we choose can be very telling about how we feel. Usually, words will be negative, positive, or neutral, giving away so much more about what one is thinking or feeling. You just need to pay attention, and you'll be able to figure them out. The thing you must keep in mind when it comes to choosing words, though, is that sometimes people will deliberately word things in a way that is meant to throw you off the scent of whatever it is they're really feeling. This is why when it comes to communication, non-verbal cues are just as important as the words that are used and how those words are said.

The concept of analyzing people and their behaviors can be a little confusing. To understand behaviorism, you have to first analyze the language used by a person under study. Behaviorists are interested in the relationship between language and behavior. According to this personality theory, every action has an emotion attached to it, such as happiness or fear. The feelings can be either positive or negative, which will have different effects on the behaviors of a subject in the study. Psychologists and behavioral experts have methods to identify positive and negative words in a person's language choices.

Certain distinctive features of language make it easy to distinguish between the two-word types, such as valence, arousal level, tense, metaphor, etc. By analyzing the way of communication through words or phrases, we can identify if a particular behavior is positive or negative. The analysis of word choice is known as the use of linguistic markers. It can be done using computers as well. Words used to describe a particular thing, action, or situation are known as evaluative words. An evaluative word is of two types, positive or negative. Positive words are those that praise something, while negative words criticize it. Positive and negative words can be linguistically analyzed to identify the behavioral patterns of a person under study and to figure out their actual emotions and intentions as they communicate with others.

Tips for Decoding Verbal Behavior

Today's society is quick to pick up on nonverbal cues. Still, sometimes the best indicators of what a person might think are their *actual words*. Verbal clues can often help you decipher someone's true feelings and intentions. Here are tips to keep in mind when decoding verbal behavior:

1. The words they say are almost always meant to persuade you of a specific feeling or experience. Almost everyone says things to themselves *out loud* as they think about what they will say next, especially when trying to persuade someone else. I.E., "to be honest," and "I really believe that..."

2. Considering the context of the situation, some say things to convince themselves that what they're feeling isn't *really* as bad as it feels. For example, someone might say, "I'm not so bad off," when they are, in fact, upset about something. Others try to convince themselves that it's all good and normal for them to be sad.

3. When someone tries to convince you of a particular feeling or experience, they will often exaggerate. They might say, "I'm really struggling here," when, in appearance, they seem just fine.

4. People often say things to avoid conflict or make themselves seem like a victim (or that they are *always* in the right.)

5. People often say things to try and make a joke or to invoke laughter in others. We will discuss how to interpret jokes and why people say them.

6. People often say things that are designed to change a topic of conversation or redirect attention to something else. We will discuss how people do this and also talk about some of your own verbal tendencies as you decode somebody else's words.

7. People will often say things to express anger rather than to try and resolve a dispute or problem. We will discuss cues and why these types of statements are often made.

8. People will sometimes say things for no reason, just because they want to fill the room's silence.

You can already clearly see that it's not enough to go on just words alone. So, in the next chapter, we're going to talk about how you can supplement what you pick up from them verbally so that you can have a well-rounded idea of what they really mean and who the person using them is truly like.

Chapter 4: Picking Up on Non-Verbal Cues

Communication with non-verbal cues involves sending various types of information or expressing attitudes and feelings without using words. This involves using body language to send particular messages, including facial expressions, general body posture, and breathing, to name a few. Non-verbal communication offers more meaning, detail, and signals than verbal communication.

"The Expression of the Emotions in Man and Animals," a book published by Charles Darwin in 1871, led to scientific research on non-verbal communication and behavior. Unspoken communication and behavior have been studied extensively since that time. Researchers have identified several types of non-verbal communication, even though these signals are often so subtle that we aren't consciously aware of them.

In this chapter, we'll discuss how non-verbal cues play a significant role in communicating, whether we realize it or not. We will then go through the different types of non-verbal cues and how you can recognize them for yourself.

Non-Verbal Communication

Non-verbal communication is the process by which people exchange ideas, information, and feelings in spoken or unspoken words. It refers to how we communicate without using words and is also known as body language. Our non-verbal communication skills reveal a lot about us and how we feel about other people and situations and are a universal language understood by all humans regardless of culture or background. Understanding non-verbal cues allow us to respond appropriately in different social scenarios, build trust more easily, recognize insincere people more quickly, and strengthen connections with friends, family members, colleagues, and romantic partners.

In other words, non-verbal communication is the delivery of unspoken messages through body language.

Non-verbal communication occurs when something other than words is used to communicate, and it can be defined as follows:

Amplitude and Frequency of Gestures

- Using space, body language, and paralanguage (gestures, tone, pitch of voice, and facial expressions) – non-verbal cues transfer meaning
- Hand placement when speaking in public
- Eye contact
- Besides written or spoken words, it includes body motion, voice characteristics, body motion, space separation, and appearance
- Shifting weight when standing
- Blinking frequency
- Communication using non-linguistic means
- The transmission of a message through a medium other than writing or speech
- Leaning forward versus sitting up
- Body posture while standing

Why Is Non-Verbal Communication Important?

We all tend to make assumptions about people, leading to snap judgments and misreading situations. Luckily, there are non-verbal cues that can help us get to know someone better and avoid assuming the worst about them.

To effectively read body language, we must first be aware of our own body language. Understanding body language and interpreting nonverbal cues are the most effective way to do this. With the help of non-verbal communication skills, we can drastically improve our social interactions and relationships, as well as help us build stronger connections, making it easier to read people and figure out their intentions.

The ability to communicate non-verbally is important at every stage of life, our workplace, personal relationships, and social situations. Having them helps us make appropriate judgments about situations. You can communicate more effectively through non-verbal communication skills in the following ways:

Reveal Personality

Communicating non-verbally helps you convey your personality. When you smile and make friendly gestures frequently, you might be perceived as a kindhearted and optimistic person.

Communicate Feelings

Non-verbal communication can be used to convey anger, happiness, annoyance, relief, disappointment, and many other emotions.

Promote Your Messages

When you use non-verbal communication skills, you can emphasize and structure what you say. For example, hand gestures or pointing could indicate to your listener that what you're saying is important.

Convey Messages

The use of non-verbal communication can help you convey messages without using verbal cues. A nod indicates agreement with what someone just said, for example.

Provide Support

Some actions assist in offering support because they speak louder than words. There are many ways to show appreciation, such as patting someone on the back or giving them a wink.

Show a Desire

To signal a preferred action, you can raise your hand when you have an idea or move closer to the door when you want to leave.

De-Escalate Tension

Conflict resolution can be helped by non-verbal communication cues such as open body language, kind smiles, calm voices, and many others.

Communicate Intention

In non-verbal communication, you can convey certain information about your feelings, whether intentionally or unintentionally. A serious frown, for example, might reveal your frustration.

Types of Non-Verbal Cues

Now that you have a better idea of how non-verbal cues affect how our communication is perceived by others, let's take a look at the seven types of non-verbal cues you should focus on when analyzing someone´s non-verbal behavior.

Facial Expressions

Usually, facial expressions unintentionally convey information and emotions. Your eyes, lips, eyebrows, and face can all be used to accomplish this. When you are excited, you may open your eyes wider and raise your eyebrows. The movement and condition of our facial muscles enable the non-verbal communication of feelings, thoughts, and actions. Generally, we can interpret a person's state of mind by looking at their body language, which reflects their internal emotions. Movements of the face communicate just as loud as words. A person's facial expressions are useful for an essential part of social interactions.

Expressions on the face cannot be viewed in isolation. In addition to the nose, eyebrows, chin, nose, and mouth, different facial features are fundamental to forming an expression. Additionally, there are adjustments to the body and head.

There are many things we can learn from a person's expression, including:

- How comfortable or uncomfortable are interactions for them?
- A person's degree of engagement
- A controlled or natural reaction to a stimulus
- Sending and interpreting communications
- Whether an individual wants to continue or discontinue interactions with another

The face is also a primary means of communicating emotions. Based on our ability to read facial expressions, we can respond appropriately to others' feelings.

The meanings of facial expressions are culturally specific and must be understood within the context of the expression. Like spoken languages, facial expressions are primarily acquired and regulated by the mind.

The simplest type of unspoken language is through expressions on the face. This allows people to develop perceptions of someone's reliability, kindness, and authority. The following are the basic categories that represent basic human emotions across cultures, according to researchers who have attempted to categorize facial expressions that express emotion:

- Sadness
- Anger
- Fear
- Disgust
- Happiness
- Surprise
- Contempt

According to the research conducted in 2021, which described the existence of universal facial expressions, we may share a total of 16 facial expressions.

- Surprise
- Amusement
- Pain
- Anger
- Elation
- Awe
- Disappointment
- Concentration
- Contentment
- Contempt
- Desire
- Doubt
- Confusion
- Interest
- Sadness
- Triumph

By practicing the use of facial expressions matching the emotions of other people, you will be able to become better at recognizing their true feelings and thoughts.

Facial Expressions Based on Facial Features

To interpret what each expression means, we tend to focus on different areas of our faces when interpreting non-verbal information. For example, a person's mouth and eyes can tell whether they are angry, happy, or sad.

Eyes

There is a common belief that eyes are windows to the soul and that we often use them to judge how others feel by watching their eyes:

- Dilation (arousal or interest)
- Diverting gaze (distraction or discomfort)
- Blinking quickly (discomfort or distress)
- Staring intensely (anger or attention)
- Blinking too little (indicating an attempt to control one's eyes)

Eyebrows

Raised eyebrows convey surprise.
https://www.pexels.com/photo/man-in-red-button-up-shirt-3777931/

Additionally, eyebrows can be used as a tool for expressing emotions, and they can play a role in facial recognition just as much as eyes do:

- Knitted together and drawn down (fear, anger, or sadness)
- Inner corners are drawn up (sadness)
- Arched and raised (surprise)

Mouth

The mouth is capable of conveying a lot more than just a smile. It is very common for people to mask their true emotions with their mouths; for example, by using a forced smile, they can hide their true feelings with their eyes' micro-expressions:

- Pursed lips (distaste)
- A dropped jaw (surprise)
- Downward-facing corners (sadness)
- Raised corners (happiness)
- Covering the mouth (hiding something)
- One side of the mouth raised (contempt or hate)
- Open mouth (fear)
- Lip biting (fear or anxiety)

Head and Neck Signals

The gestures you make with your neck and head are much more important than you might think.

As soon as we meet someone, the first thing we notice about them is their head (especially their face). Therefore, it is crucial to understand the signals our heads and necks send to other people.

The Neck

The neck dimple (suprasternal notch) is the area in which your collarbones meet. It may be an attempt to calm jitters or worry if someone rubs this area because it reduces our pulse and relaxes us.

The following cues can also help you determine a person's emotional state:

- Elongated or exposed neck (vulnerability or flirting)
- Scratching neck (disagreement or uncertain)
- Noticeable, throbbing neck vein (anxious, angry, stressed, or fearful)

Head Gestures

The majority of people will nod or shake their heads when they are asked a question. Also, when greeting each other from a distance, it is customary to use a slight head nod. You might be surprised to learn head movements can convey many different unconscious signals.

- You will earn the trust of your audience by tilting your head while you speak
- Nodding rapidly (unwilling to listen)
- One-sided head tilt (skepticism, curiosity, apprehension)
- Nodding slowly (interested and attentive)

Chin Positions

In a horizontal posture, the chin is neutral, but in the following position:

- Pulled back and down (condemning, displeased, or aggressive). Partially conceals the neck's vulnerable front section
- Raised vertically (smugness, courage, or pride)
- In a horizontal position (sad or timid), one subconsciously diminishes their position and stature by doing so.

We understand non-verbal cues from head movements because they are rich in communication. Western cultures tend to nod their head when agreeing, for example. Or, during a meeting, we gauge participant interest and understanding via their head movements. We know an audience understands and is interested if they nod. In contrast, if their heads move around, we get the impression that they are bored or uninterested.

General Body Postures

We can communicate our subconscious thoughts and emotions through our movements and general body postures. Folding your arms, crossing your legs, sitting, standing, walking, using your hips and eyes, and even moving your lips are examples of this. Our body language speaks louder than words and can involve behaviors such as:

- Rubbing the eyes
- Touching the nose
- Pausing while we speak
- Clearing the throat
- Wearing certain clothes
- Using certain scents

For example, pressing the index finger to your lips can indicate that you want people to be quiet. Constantly wearing baggy clothes can convey a lack of self-esteem. Someone biting their nails, fidgeting with something in their hands, or shaking their knee may express nervousness, disinterest, or boredom.

Appearance

Additionally, we silently convey information through our outfits, haircuts, and colors. Research in color psychology suggests that various colors can evoke specific emotions. Think about your tendency to judge people by their physical characteristics. First impressions play a major factor in our social interactions. This is why job seekers are compelled to dress appropriately for prospective job interviews.

Our clothing can reveal a lot about ourselves, such as our personality, profession, status, and nationality. The clothes people wear may affect their reactions according to their class and stage of life.

A person's appearance is largely determined by their culture. While Western societies tend to favor slim bodies, some ethnic groups in Africa view large body shapes as a sign of prosperity.

Chest and Shoulder Signals

Our posture speaks volumes about how we present ourselves and respond to others in conversation. A head held high and rounded back shoulders can communicate confidence when conversing while standing. On the other hand, when sitting, an arched back, crossing of arms, and slouching postures may suggest an unreceptive or uninterested signal. Although we seek comfortable positions, especially when talking for a long time, bad postural habits often occur naturally.

Gestures and Handshakes

There are several ways in which the gestures of the hands punctuate the spoken word and can provide valuable context for the speaker and what they are saying. It is sometimes possible to distinguish a speaker's emotional state from hand gestures.

Common deliberate or subconscious gestures or signals can convey meaning without words:

- Pointing
- Waving

- Using fingers to indicate numeric amounts
- Animated hand gestures while speaking could indicate passion or excitement
- Trembling hands could mean dishonesty or anxiety

Using non-verbal cues is quite common in the courtroom. Attorneys have utilized non-verbal signals to persuade jurors to support their side of the argument. To undermine the credibility of a witness, a lawyer might glance at their watch to convey contempt at the opposing argument. In courtrooms, some judges even limit what type of non-verbal behavior is allowed due to the powerful influence of these non-verbal signals.

Both our professional and personal lives can benefit from strong communication skills. The importance of verbal and written communication cannot be overstated. Still, non-verbal behaviors comprise a significant portion of our daily interpersonal communication.

Breathing

Researchers at Oslo University have found that sighing is a form of non-verbal communication, whether subconscious or not. In most cases, a sigh is a non-verbal communication of negativity like sadness or impatience. When you sigh or hear a sigh, it is important to recognize its meaning.

In a series of studies, the University of Oslo examined the interpretation and motivation of sighs and concluded:

- Sighing is interpreted as frustration
- Sighing is associated with negative emotions
- Private and public sighs are equally frequent, suggesting a subconscious mechanism

Other forms of non-verbal cues include:

- Deep and slow breathing indicates a self-soothing technique used with anxious or stressed
- Taking deep breaths is often a sign of elation
- As the lungs prepare for flight or fight, deep breathing can also be a sign of anger
- A shallow breathing pattern indicates physical or emotional arousal

Physical Movements

A great deal of information can also be conveyed by body movement. Arm-crossings, leg crosses, and defensive postures have been over-interpreted in popular media. While it is true that body language conveys emotions and opinions, studies indicate that non-verbal cues are far more nuanced and ambiguous compared to what was previously believed.

A person's body movements can range from swaying to nodding to using their hands when talking and everything in between. Talking about a subject may be expressed through certain body postures, such as flailing your hands. In contrast, your body movements may occur unconsciously, so try being mindful of how your actions might affect your listener. For example, other movements, such as swaying back and forth, are distracting and can undermine your message during a presentation.

Use of Space (Proxemics)

It may be because the other person stood in too close proximity whenever you feel uncomfortable, even while talking. Physical space is a need we all have, though the needs vary depending on culture, situation, and relationship closeness. The use of physical space serves as a means of conveying affection, hostility, and control without words.

The physical distance between people can set the tone for the conversation. If you're with friends and one of them approaches you while you're on the other side of the room, this may indicate they have something confidential to say. In other cases, touching someone or getting too close to them as you speak might be considered hostile or intrusive.

The need for personal space is also an effective way of communicating non-verbally.

The amount of distance we need and the amount of space we perceive belongs to us are influenced by many different factors:

- Cultural expectations
- Social norms
- Situational factors
- Familiarity level
- Personality traits

Various cultures require different distances of personal space, according to studies found in the Journey of Cross-Cultural Psychology:

Romania: Stranger (4.6 feet), personal acquaintance (3.1 feet)
Norway: Stranger (3.4 feet), personal acquaintance (2.4 feet)
Mexico: Stranger (3.3 feet), personal acquaintance (2.7 feet)
United States: Stranger (3.1 feet), personal acquaintance (2,3 feet)
Argentina: Stranger (2.5 feet), personal acquaintance (2 feet)

Humans are born with a natural tendency to express emotions, and we use our bodies as tools for communication. We tend to rely on non-verbal cues more than verbal ones, especially when communicating emotions. Facial expressions especially can convey a great deal of information about a person's thoughts and feelings. Sometimes, we may not even know the physical signals that convey our emotions.

As you can see, non-verbal communication plays an important role in human interaction. As such, it is vital to understand its importance and how to use it effectively. Become conscious of your own mannerisms to become more adept at communicating through non-verbal cues. You can do this by learning to read body language and other non-verbal signals. In addition, you can help others make better decisions when they use non-verbal communication skills.

Chapter 5: Understanding Different Personality Types

People don't come with a manual that instructs you on the best way to interact with them or what to do when they are angry or why they lie. Only when you truly know someone will you begin to unravel all the different aspects and layers of their personality. One of the things that we usually struggle with is understanding why people lie to us or deceive us. In fact, lying comes as second nature for some people, and it always amazes those around them how they can lie with such ease. To understand the motive behind certain behaviors, we must first understand other people's personalities and their most dominant traits. Although people don't come with manuals, each person falls under a specific personality type.

In the mid-20th century in the USA, a woman called Katharine Cook Briggs and her daughter Isabel Briggs Myers were influenced by psychiatrist Carl Jung's research, especially "Psychological Types." Inspired by his work, Katherine and Isabel worked together to create a list of questions that their answers would determine a person's personality type. In 1962, the Myers-Briggs Type Indicator, or MBTI instrument, came to life. To this day, people use this tool to determine their personality and better understand themselves and the people in their lives. This chapter will cover the Myers-Briggs 16 personality types and their traits.

The Myers-Briggs 16 Personality Types

ISTJ (The Inspector)

I
Introversion
S
Sensing
T
Thinking
J
Judging

ISTJ individuals may initially seem intimidating and unapproachable because of their serious and formal demeanor. They are old souls who highly value traditions and are very cultured. ISTJs focus on the details in every situation, which is why they are referred to as inspectors. They are *not* rule-breakers and are usually attuned to the logical side of their brain, which they use to achieve their goals. Their dominant trait is introverted sensing which allows them to pay attention to the details, while their extraverted thinking drives them to think logically and efficiently. Their social circle is small, and they are extremely loyal to their family and friends. These individuals prefer jobs that require logical thinking, stability, and structure, like engineering, architecture, management, finance, and social science.

Traits
- Well-respected
- Organized
- Detail-oriented
- Intellectual
- Traditional
- Calm
- Responsible
- Hard-working
- Honorable
- Quiet

- Reserved
- Serious
- Stubborn
- Committed, especially in relationships

INFJ (The Counselor)
I
Introversion
N
Intuition
F
Feeling
J
Judging

INFJs see the world differently as a result of their idealistic nature. They are inspectors who would rather search, analyze, and dig deep than take things at face value. For this reason, they are often misunderstood by those around them, and some people may consider them weird. However, this hasn't stopped them from being deep thinkers who gravitate toward complex topics. They often come up with the best ideas because they are visionaries, imaginative, and very creative. These individuals can find inspiration in everything, which is the reason behind their creativity. They work well with a team because they don't like conflict and prefer to cooperate with others instead.

For this reason, they are referred to as diplomats. Their dominant trait is introverted intuition, which greatly impacts their decision-making process and makes them pay attention to internal insights. Their extraverted feeling trait is what makes them empathetic toward other people's feelings. In relationships, they crave harmony and intimacy and are very supportive. They will thrive in jobs requiring teamwork, psychology, and compassion, like a physiatrist, counselor, or teacher.

Traits
- Visionaries
- Passionate, mainly about their dreams
- Structured

- Approachable
- Caring
- Warm
- Usually follow their gut feelings
- Cautious
- Helpful
- Sensitive
- Tactful
- Empathic
- Compassionate
- Practical
- Decisive
- Private

INTJ (The Mastermind)

I
Introversion
N
Intuition
T
Thinking
J
Judging

INTJ individuals are introverts by nature. They find spending time alone to be more peaceful since people usually drain their energy which is why they need to recharge after socializing. INTJs enjoy their own company and are very comfortable in their own skin. They are very quiet and reserved and prefer to work solo than in a team. Strategic and innovative, they are usually the ones to come up with the best strategies and plans, whether at work or in any situation. They excel at solving problems as a result of their analytical nature. INTJs aren't the ones to sit and discuss the weather since they find small talk and boring conversations to be tedious. They would rather discuss theories or interesting ideas instead. While many believe that everything happens for a reason, INTJs are often curious about this reason. Their dominant trait is introverted intuition, allowing them to analyze patterns and read between the lines. While their extraverted thinking is what is responsible for their organizational skills. They are extremely loyal in relationships and their partners' biggest cheerleaders. They prefer careers where they can use their innovative skills and logical thinking, like architects, civil engineers, surgeons, computer programmers, and lawyers.

Traits
- Ambitious
- Detached
- Reserved
- Rational
- Ruthless
- Logical
- The ability to understand even the most complex theories
- Perfectionists, especially in their professional lives
- Intuitive
- Insightful
- Innovative
- Determined

ENFJ (The Giver)
E
Extraversion
N
Intuition
F
Feeling
J
Judging

Unlike INTJs, ENFJs are extroverted by nature and are even considered people-pleasers. People also enjoy the company of ENFJs since they are charismatic and outspoken. They can easily connect with others, even those who are different from them. They rely more on their feelings and intuition when making decisions than logical thinking. ENFJs are highly imaginative and aren't keen on living in the real world. They aren't concerned with the present moment and are often focused on future possibilities and abstracts. ENFJs are empaths who can feel what other people are feeling. Their main trait is an extraverted feeling responsible for their empathetic nature. At the same time, their introverted intuition makes them more focused on the future than the here and now. ENFJs are extremely supportive and understanding of their partners. They prefer careers that motivate and encourage others, like teachers, marriage therapists, human resources managers, and psychologists.

Traits
- Idealistic
- Ethical
- Open-minded
- Accepting
- Kind
- Loyal
- Reliable
- Good communication skills
- Passionate
- Organized
- Inability to handle uncertainties
- Generous
- People pleasers
- Caring
- Warm
- Persuasive
- Natural leaders
- Indecisive

ISTP (The Craftsman)

I
Introversion

S
Sensing

T
Thinking

P
Perceiving

Many people usually misunderstand ISTPs mainly because of their mysterious personalities. ISTPs have two slides to their personalities. They can be rational and logical, yet they can also be very unpredictable and spontaneous. However, most people only get to see the rational side of their personality since ISTPs rarely show their true nature to anyone. Their dominant trait is introverted thinking, allowing them to use logic when dealing with each situation. Their extraverted sensing is what makes them more focused on the abstract. They are very calm in relationships and prefer to take care of all the handy work around the house. Like their name, the craftsman, they prefer careers that rely on physical activities like mechanics, firefighters, carpenters, and chefs, or technical jobs like software developers, financial planners, or system analysts.

Traits

- Focused on the present moment
- Risk-takers
- Determined
- Independent
- Easy-going
- Laid back
- Realistic
- Practical
- Problem solvers
- Fair
- Flexible

- Creative
- Logical
- Impatient
- Private
- Insensitive

ESFJ (The Provider)

E
Extraversion
S
Sensing
F
Feeling
J
Judging

ESFJs are extremely extroverted individuals. They love socializing and being around people. They are very popular, and people enjoy their company because they know how to lift others' spirits and make them feel good about themselves. ESFJs are born to be under the spotlight. As teenagers, they were often popular in high school, and as adults, their popularity hasn't slowed down. They are often the ones throwing parties to bring together their family and friends. It's no wonder that everyone likes them. ESFJ's dominant trait is an extroverted feeling which makes them rely more on their gut feeling, while their introverted senses make them only focused on the here and now. ESFJs are very traditional and prefer stable relationships. They prefer careers where they can use their interpersonal skills, like receptionists, teachers, nurses, and counselors.

Traits

- Social butterflies
- Extroverted
- Sociable
- Realistic
- Sensitive
- Helpful

- Energetic
- Great listeners
- Warm and genuine
- Popular
- Organized
- Empathetic
- Compassionate

INFP (The Idealist)
I
Introversion
N
Intuition
F
Feeling
P
Perceiving

Out of all the personality types, INFPs are the most introverted. They are reserved and quiet and would rather spend time alone in a quiet setting than socialize with a group of people. They need peace and quiet to simply sit with their thoughts and try to make sense of everything that is going on around them. They pay so much attention to signs and believe there is a deeper meaning behind everything they see. They will often contemplate trying to find the meaning behind them. Daydreamers, these individuals are often lost in their thoughts and imaginations. Their dominant trait is an introverted feeling which allows them to only feel and process their emotions on the inside. At the same time, their extraverted intuition helps them deal with various situations through their imagination. In relationships, they have no problem compromising when it comes to someone they care about. However, they are very selective when it comes to choosing their friends. They usually thrive in careers like writing, photography, teaching preschools, and librarians.

Traits
- Dedicated
- Idealistic

- Sensitive
- Vulnerable
- Selfless
- Mediators
- Avoid Conflicts
- Loves and enjoys life
- Cares about other people's feelings
- Controlling
- Spontaneous
- Flexible
- Warm
- Compassionate
- Perceptive and Intuitive

ESFP (The Performer)

E
Extraversion
S
Sensing
F
Feeling
P
Perceptive

ESFP are born to be in the spotlight. For this reason, they are referred to as entertainers. They are the funny and entertaining ones in the group. They amuse others and enjoy it when all the attention is on them. ESFPs are always looking out for new things to learn because they want to use their interpersonal skills to share what they have learned with others. They are so much fun to be around and are the life of the party. Although they may seem eager to hog the spotlight, they are, in fact, very warm, friendly, and generous individuals. They are the first to ask someone if they are OK as they are naturally sympathetic. Their extraverted sensing makes them focus on facts rather than abstract ideas, while their introverted feeling helps them with decision-making. Regarding relationships, nothing comes before their loved ones and their family. These entertainers prefer careers that rely on spontaneity and artistic values, like musicians, artists, fashion designers, and florists.

Traits
- Positive
- Supportive
- Bold
- Showmanship
- Practical
- Poor attention span
- Sensitive
- Easily bored
- Entertainers
- Strong interpersonal skills
- Lives in the present moment
- Sympathetic
- Generous
- Warm

ENFP (The Champion)

E

Extraversion

N

Intuition

F

Feeling

P

Perceiving

ENFPs are known for their individualism and live their lives outside the box. They are born to lead, not to follow, and do things their own way and follow their own ideas and beliefs with no concerns for the status quo. They enjoy spending time with like-minded individuals and prefer people who are as intuitive as them. ENTPs let themselves be guided by their feelings rather than their mind, which usually works for them since they are highly perceptive. Their extraverted intuition makes them more focused on abstract patterns and thoughts, while their introverted feelings are what make them rely on emotions rather than logical thinking. These individuals are usually very affectionate and expressive in relationships. ENFPs prefer jobs where they can be imaginative and creative, like authors, actors, dancers, or art directors.

Traits
- Thoughtful
- Highly perceptive
- Natural-born leaders
- Strong communication skills
- Overthinkers
- Hypersensitive
- Overemotional
- Focused on the future
- Genuine Warm
- Isn't keen on authority figures
- Empathetic
- Hates routine
- Enjoys socializing

ESTP (The Doer)
E
Extraversion
S
Sensing
T
Thinking
P
Perceiving

ESTPs are typical extroverts who thrive around people and never say no to an event or a social gathering. They are free-thinkers, yet they also use reason and logical thinking. Theories and abstract ideas are of no interest to them. They are risk-takers and spontaneous and jump without looking. Mistakes don't scare them, as they don't let them get in their way. They will simply deal with them when they occur. Their extraverted sensing is what drives them to take action right away. At the same time, their introverted thinking allows them to be observant and disciplined. In relationships, they are fun and spontaneous and enjoy going on adventures with their loved ones. They prefer adventurous and flexible careers like firefighters, military officers, police officers, and pilots.

Traits
- Bold
- Sociable
- Direct
- Impatient
- Judgmental
- Commitment issues
- Unstructured
- Great people skills
- Dramatic
- Adventurous
- Risk-takers
- Enjoys the spotlight
- Fun personality

ESTJ (The Supervisor)
E
Extraversion
S
Sensing
T
Thinking
J
Judging

ESTJs are extremely traditional individuals. They live their lives by doing what is right and what society deems acceptable. They are often the perfect citizens doing the right thing, no matter the cost. As a result of their responsible personality, people often seek their advice and guidance, and an ESTJ is always more than happy to help. They are usually more practical than other personality types due to their extraverted thinking, while their introverted sense makes them stable individuals who are focused on details. They are very reliable and often come through for their loved ones in relationships. ESTJs prefer leadership positions like chefs, sales managers, office managers, and school principals.

Traits
- Organized
- Dedicated
- Committed
- Efficient
- Inflexible
- Workaholic
- Stubborn
- Judgmental
- Responsible
- Dignified
- Practical
- Traditional
- Hardworking
- Loyal
- Highly ethical

ENTJ (The Commander)
E
Extraversion
N
Intuition
T
Thinking
J

Judging

ENTJs are extremely logical and rational individuals who handle anything that comes their way with great discipline. Their leadership skills surpass any other of the 16 personality types. Whether it is their personal or professional lives, they are always the first ones to jump in and take charge. These individuals make things happen for themselves instead of waiting around for something to happen. They don't see obstacles as something to hold them back but more as challenges to push them to keep going. Making decisions usually comes easily to them. Their extraverted intuition allows them to be calculated regarding orders and judgments.

In contrast, their introverted intuition makes them rely on their instincts when making a decision. They can be controlling in their relationships and may have high expectations for their partners. ENTJs prefer complex careers that require strategies, like logisticians, financial analysts, aerospace engineers, and economists.

Traits

- Strategic thinkers
- Charismatic
- Strong-willed
- Efficient
- Arrogant
- Intolerant
- Blunt
- Dominant
- Self-confident
- Natural-born leaders
- Strong communication skills
- Focused
- Perfectionist
- Logical

INTP (The Thinker)

I
Introversion

N
Intuitive

T
Thinking

P
Perceiving

INTPs are extremely brilliant and logical individuals. They can easily see patterns and notice if something isn't right or out of place. It is almost impossible to lie to an INTP because they can read people. They prefer flexible environments where they can be creative, away from structure and routine. Thanks to their introverted thinking, they are deep thinkers, while their extraverted intuition is what drives their imaginative skills. They are extremely independent and unconventional in relationships. They prefer flexible and non-traditional careers like writers, photographers, composers, and directors.

Traits

- Imaginative
- Objective
- Enthusiastic
- Insensitive
- Condescending
- Absent-minded
- Easy-going
- Laid-back
- Logical
- Unconventional
- Independent
- Values knowledge

ISFJ (The Nurturer)

I
Introversion

S
Sensing

F
Feeling

J
Judging

ISFJs are true nurturers who are generous and want to help others. If they believe in a cause or a person, they will follow and support them with great enthusiasm and selflessness. They are empaths who are extremely sensitive to other people's feelings and needs. People love them because they are considerate and bring out the best in them. Their introverted sense makes them focused on details, while their extraverted sense influences their nurturing quality. They provide unconditional love and care to their loved ones. They prefer careers with structure and where they can work away from the spotlight, like social workers, dentists, tellers, or personal financial advisors.

Traits

- Kind-hearted
- Warm
- Supportive
- Practical
- Hard-working
- Honorable
- Resistant to change
- Dependable
- Non-confrontational
- Stable
- Down to earth
- Workaholics

ENTP (The Visionary)
E
Extraversion
N
Intuition
T
Thinking
P
Perceiving

ENTP is one of the rarest personalities. They are extroverts; however, they dislike small talk and don't usually enjoy social situations. In fact, if they are surrounded by people who are different from them, ENTPs will most likely want to leave. They thrive on knowledge and are considered very intelligent individuals. During arguments or heated conversations, they are usually rational and logical. They prefer to discuss theories and facts instead of having idle conversations. Their extraverted intuition pushes them to learn and explore new ideas, while their extroverted thinking makes them logical thinkers. ENTPs are usually very exciting and spontaneous in relationships. They prefer challenging and creative careers like acting, translation, editing, or advertising.

Traits
- Confident
- Brave
- Innovative
- Adaptable
- Impractical
- Procrastinator
- Non-conformist
- Great social skills
- Charming
- Smart
- Creative
- Highly knowledgeable

- Creative

ISFP (The Composer)

I
Introversion

S
Sensing

F
Feeling

P
Perceiving

Although ISFPs are introverts, they don't always seem like it. At first, they may struggle a little to connect with other people. However, once you get to know them, you will find them friendly and great fun to be around. They are the friend you can make exciting plans with or call to do something new or spontaneous, and they will jump at the opportunity. They live in the moment and know how to enjoy themselves. Unlike most introverts, this personality type enjoys meeting new people. They are very caring individuals as a result of their introverted feeling. Their extraverted sensing is what makes them enjoy art. They are very flexible and easy-going in relationships; they prefer jobs that don't put them in the spotlight, like artists, mechanics, graphic designers, and geologists.

Traits

- Spontaneous
- Approachable
- Warm
- Friendly
- Bold
- Observant
- Unpredictable
- Sensitive
- Indecisive
- Serious
- Disciplined

- Considerate
- Tactful
- Free-spirited
- Adventurous

Quiz

Now that you know about the 16 Myers-Briggs personality types, it is time to figure out which one you are. We are going to present you with two opposing sides. By the end of this quiz, you can calculate your results based on the choices you made and determine your personality type.

Are you more of an introvert or an extrovert? Take note of only the answers that apply to you.

Extroversion (E)
- I have many friends and different interests
- I take action pretty fast
- I speak before I think
- I am usually the one that initiates conversations
- I am sociable
- I am more focused on the outside world
- I get more energetic after socializing

Introversion (I)
- I have a few deep friendships and refined interests
- I take my time before taking action
- I think before I speak
- I wait for others to approach me to start a conversation
- I am usually quite
- I am more focused on my inner world
- Spending time with people drains me, and I recharge when I am alone

How do you view the world?

Sensors (S)
- I prefer doing things the traditional way
- I am very observant
- I am a doer
- I enjoy practical things
- I usually think in concrete terms
- I am focused on the here and now
- I pay attention to details
- I am attuned to all my senses

Intuitive (N)
- I prefer doing things using new ideas
- I am imaginative and creative
- I am a dreamer
- I enjoy theories
- I usually think in abstract terms
- I focus on the future and what could be
- I am focused on the big picture
- I follow my gut feeling (sixth sense)

What is your decision-making process?

Thinkers (T)
- I take a more scientific approach
- I am fair and treat everyone equally
- I am interested in things and ideas
- I use logic to make decisions
- I use my head

Feelers (F)
- I take a more poetic approach
- I am compassionate and treat people based on their situation
- I am more interested in people and emotions
- My decisions are based on my values

- I use my heart

What is your planning process?

Judgers (J)
- I am eager to make a final decision
- I prefer to be in control of my life
- I stick to the plan
- I plan ahead
- I am structured and organized

Perceivers (P)
- I am always looking for more information
- I let life happen
- I adapt easily
- I go with the flow
- I am relaxed and casual

If you checked more answers under introverts, then you have the I. In the next question, if you check more answers under the sensors, you have the S, and so on. By the end, you will have the four letters that will determine your personality.

Chapter 6: The Why Behind Lies

Why do people lie? You have probably asked yourself this question on more than one occasion. A person would look you dead in the eye and tell you a fabricated story, and you wonder how they are able to do this with such ease. If you don't understand how people can lie so easily, then you probably fall under the personality types that don't lie. There were various studies conducted on this topic to find out why people lie. Scholars have found that there is a link between an individual's personality type and their ability to lie. Among the 16 personality types that we have discussed in the previous chapter, some are better at lying and deceiving than others.

According to a study conducted at the University of Tennessee, each person has a motive to lie, which is usually based on their personality type. The study also stated that there are different ways people go about lying. We usually consider lying to be providing false information. However, omitting certain important details, exaggerating the truth, or distorting the truth are all considered forms of lying and deception. People's motives for lying differ. Some lie to benefit themselves, while there are others who lie to strangers but never to close family or friends. This shows that most people are aware that they are lying and consciously choose whom to lie to and whom to be honest with.

The study also shows that there are several reasons that motivate people to lie. People may lie to avoid embarrassing themselves, to protect themselves from harmful situations, to protect their privacy, to protect someone they care about, to get out of an unpleasant situation, to get a reward, to look good in front of others, to avoid consequences or punishment, or to showcase their power. While some of these motives may be admirable, like protecting others, there are other motives that are based on deception. That said, not all lies fall under these categories. For instance, there are white lies that we tell people to be polite – perhaps about how their food tastes good or their home looks nice. These lies are necessary to spare others' feelings and to avoid poor manners.

There are two types of people, those who find it easy to lie and deceive and those who are easily deceived. This mainly depends on a person's personality type. We will explore in this chapter the Myer-Briggs personality types that can lie with ease and the motives behind their actions, and the personality types which can be easily deceived. It is essential to note that not every personality type we mention here will lie and deceive the same way. Each personality type has a dark side, but not everyone is in touch with this dark side. So be careful before making judgments and consider the other factors we mentioned in this book.

MBTI Types Most Likely to Deceive

According to a study conducted by social psychologist and author Bella DePaulo, extroverts usually lie more than introverts. We aren't saying that extroverts are liars or bad people. They simply interact with people more and talk more than introverts, providing them with more opportunities to lie. Social niceties also factor in, as extroverts may have to tell small lies during a conversation or a social interaction to avoid awkward situations or hurting someone's feelings. In fact, most extroverts aren't aware that they are lying as most of these "simple lies" come naturally to them or consider them part of a normal conversation. Unlike introverts, extroverts don't think before they speak, and they may end up saying things they don't mean or exaggerating the truth. They may also lie during job interviews and on job applications. It isn't clear what motives drive extroverts to lie, but according to various research, these individuals may lie to be socially accepted and to win other people's admiration.

Sensor individuals may also lie since they don't usually think of the consequences of their actions. Perceivers who live in the moment and don't concern themselves with the consequences of their actions tend to lie as well. They are also witty and charming and can get out of any situation by providing false information. Feeling individuals can be people pleasers and may lie to spare people's feelings or impress them.

The quiet and reserved introvert is usually more trustworthy. They are calm, neutral, and don't say much. However, they mean what they say when they speak, making people believe them.

ESFP

Although ESFPs value honesty, they struggle with the truth sometimes. They like to keep the peace in their relationships, so they may omit certain information to avoid "unnecessary" arguments. From their own point of view, omitting this information will make their partner happy. That said, they do feel guilty about deceiving their loved ones because they want to be open with them.

At their worst, ESFPs desire nothing more than sensation and attention. They can also be impulsive and want to be the only ones under the spotlight. If someone tries to hog the spotlight from them, they may become passive-aggressive. They can also be immature and only concerned with instant gratification. They also don't think of the consequences of their decisions. As a result, ESFP may exaggerate the truth to get attention, provide false information without thinking of the consequences, or even cheat on their partners because they are looking for thrills.

Things an ESFP May Lie About

For instance, an ESFP attended a party, and their ex-partner was there. Naturally, they won't be happy about it when their current partner finds out. To avoid an unnecessary argument, an ESFP may lie and say that they didn't know that their ex would be there. They may also leave out the part where they danced with their ex to avoid hurting their partner. Remember, they don't think of the consequences of their actions, so they just had fun with their ex without thinking about how it would affect their current partner.

ESTP

ESTPs are very private individuals and don't find it necessary to be open about everything that goes on in their lives. They can be open with the people they care about. However, they may lie or omit certain details to spare someone's feelings. ESTPs may also like to make themselves look good. They care about their image so much that if there is a piece of information that will make them look bad, they will remove this part from the story.

At their worst, ESTPs are excellent manipulators who have no problem lying or deceiving others to get their way. Morals and ethics are of no concern to them as long as they can get what they want. They are impulsive and reckless and only care about having fun, even if it is at the expense of others.

Things an ESTP May Lie About
When an ESTP is telling a story, but a part of this story will put them in a bad light, they will omit this part to protect their image.

ENTP
Similar to ESTP, ENTPs are private and struggle with opening up to people. They would rather omit certain details than be entirely truthful. In most cases, they aren't doing this to keep things from their loved ones or have any intention to lie. They just aren't comfortable with sharing personal details about themselves. At their worst, they have no problem with lying and deceiving to achieve their goals.

Things an ESTP May Lie About
ESTPs may have no problem lying to get ahead in their career. They may take credit for work or ideas that aren't theirs if it makes them look good in front of their boss and get promoted.

ENFP
Generally, ENFPs value honesty. However, they can unintentionally omit details. They either forget to provide this information, or there are certain things that they believe shouldn't be shared. At their worst, they can be manipulative, deceitful, and untrustworthy. They don't care who they deceive as long as it can get them what they want. ENFPs have no issue with taking advantage of others. In fact, they will only care about a person if they can benefit from them.

Things an ENFP May Lie About
They may pretend to like someone or befriend them to get something from them. For instance, they may become your friend, charm you, and make plans with you. You may find out later that they are doing this because they want you to finance their next project.

ISTP
Some introverts are capable of lying as well. They are also private and feel no need to share certain information with others. For this reason, they are careful about what they share and what they keep to themselves. They believe in setting boundaries and that certain people don't have the right to learn everything about them. In their careers, ISTPs usually push themselves above their limits. They may take more work than they can

handle, agree on a deadline, and don't follow through. They don't have an intention to lie or deceive others. Sometimes, they get bored and jump from one project to the next without finishing the first one. This doesn't mean that they don't keep their word; their enthusiasm may either fade away or they simply struggle to commit to a deadline.

At their worst, ISTPs have no moral compass and don't care whom they lie to or deceive in the pursuit of their pleasure or to get ahead in their career.

Things an ISTP May Lie About

If you work with an ISTP, don't expect them to finish a project on time or respect the deadline. They will get excited about a project and prepare and assure you they will have the time for it. However, they may end up finishing it a few days or even weeks late. Still, they will make up for it by delivering great results.

INTJ

INTJs believe that practicality indicates that you don't share every little detail about yourself with others. They know the difference between what they should say and what they should withhold. They don't regard this as lying or hiding the truth but as a necessity to set boundaries. However, when it comes to their romantic partners, they are more open.

At their worst, some INTJs may be narcissists who would lie, deceive, and cheat but can find the justification for it. Their narcissism blinds them and makes them believe that they can get away with things.

Things an INTJ May Lie About

The strange thing is that INTJs may lie to themselves before they lie to others. They believe they can be in control of everything, including their emotions. After working hard and getting what they want, they may still find themselves unhappy. They need to stop lying to themselves and accept the fact they aren't always in control. Getting honest with themselves, letting go, and accepting they can't control everything (especially their emotions) may be what they need.

The Dark Triad

In addition to the Myers-Briggs personality types, there are other personality types that are capable of lying, deceiving, and manipulating, referred to as the "Dark Triad." This personality type includes narcissism, psychopathy, and Machiavellianism.

Psychopathy

People who were born with psychopathic personality traits are manipulators and lack empathy. They would do anything to achieve their goals, even if it is at the expense of others. These individuals lie for the fun of it. In fact, it amuses them when they can deceive others. They may not even gain anything from lying; they just want to see if they can get away with it. People with psychopathic traits also lie to get what they want and create a grander self-image that others can admire. That said, you shouldn't confuse psychopathy with being a psychopath, which is a trait often associated with serial killers.

Narcissism

Narcissists are selfish, arrogant, and lack empathy. These individuals are dominant, entitled, and have a grandiose self-image. They often lie to keep up with this fake grandiose image they have created for themselves.

Machiavellianism

Machiavellianism was named after Niccolo Machiavelli, an Italian politician who lived in the 16th century. He authored a book titled "The Prince," which was about acquiring power by any means necessary, like using cunning methods or deceit. Machiavellianism is associated with the traits mentioned in this book, like manipulation, duplicity, and lack of empathy and morality.

These individuals often lie if it benefits them; they manipulate others, and they also tell white lies to achieve their goals.

MBTI Types Most Likely to Be Deceived

Just as there are personality types who lie and deceive, there are others who can easily be deceived. This doesn't necessarily mean that they are gullible; they are just well-intentioned and don't want to believe that someone they care about would lie to them. In this part of the chapter, we will focus on the personality types that can be deceived.

Many of us lie. We don't do it out of malice, but we may lie to avoid hurting others or just to be polite. We will also focus on the lies the rest of the personality traits may tell.

INFJ

It isn't easy to lie or deceive INFJs because they are usually skeptical. However, once they start trusting and loving someone, they will believe anything they say to the extent of questioning their own beliefs. That said, they are very selective about who they let into their lives.

Things an INFJ May Lie About

INFJs are called counselors because their friends, family, and even strangers would go to them for advice. They love to help and provide emotional support. However, they are introverts and empaths who get drained easily and absorb other people's emotions which can be exhausting. For this reason, they need some time to themselves. INFJs will always tell others they are ready to listen to them even though they don't feel like it. They lie to be there for others – but at their own expense.

INFJs are likely to offer emotional support even when they don't feel like it.
https://www.pexels.com/photo/woman-in-blue-shirt-talking-to-a-young-man-in-white-shirt-8550841/

ENFJ

When an ENFJ lets someone into their lives, they will completely trust and believe them, even when it is clear that this person isn't telling the truth.

Things an ENFJ May Lie About

ENFJs are genuine and sincere individuals who don't like lying or even omitting certain information. They find this a deal breaker if you lie to them or keep things from them.

INFP

INFP blindly trusts the people they care about. Someone can blatantly lie to them, and they would believe them because they admire them. They simply refuse to believe that a person they choose to trust can be a liar or deceitful.

Things an INFP May Lie About

INFPs are different, and they know it. The great thing about them is that they aren't looking to fit in. However, they may face situations where they will have to do things to get along with others. If you are an INFP and work with a team, and someone suggests you do something their way, you will agree. However, you know you will probably end up doing things in your own creative way, or you will feel trapped and end up making something you aren't proud of. You didn't mean to lie; you have good intentions and just wanted to get along with others. However, you are too creative and free-spirited to do things the traditional way.

ISTJ

ISTJs are skeptical by nature but would never question someone they love or trust deeply.

Things an ISTJ May Lie About

ISTJs don't lie, not even to spare someone's feelings. They are so blunt that people may find them rude or mean.

ESTJ

ESTJs don't usually believe everything people tell them, but this isn't the case with their close circle. However, if they give you their trust and you keep lying to them, they will never believe or trust you again.

Things an ESTJ May Lie About

ESTJs are honest individuals. However, they will never share their innermost feelings with anyone. This doesn't mean they aren't truthful; they just don't know how to communicate what they are feeling.

ISFJ

ISFJs are very trusting individuals, and others often take advantage of them. They believe that their loved ones or anyone in authority or a position of power would never lie to them. They believe they can trust and depend on these people and see no reason to question their motives. Even when it is obvious that someone is tricking them, they will still believe they are being sincere.

Things an ISFJ May Lie About

ISFJs are some of the nicest people you will ever meet; they only lie to spare people's feelings. They are the friend who would tell you that you lost weight when you have clearly gained a few pounds or that you look great in a hideous dress! They would never hurt someone's feelings. (While this is a nice trait, sometimes it is best to be honest and not let their friend leave the house in an ugly outfit.)

ESFJ

ESFJs can be gullible around their loved ones and believe everything they tell them. However, if you lie to them, trick them, or hurt their feelings, they will know you can't be trusted again.

Things an ESFJ May Lie About

ESFJs will only lie to their loved ones to spare their feelings. However, when it comes to strangers, they believe that certain things shouldn't be shared. For this reason, they may omit details or information from them. They are just private individuals who don't believe in sharing everything with strangers.

ISFP

ISFPs trust the people they let into their lives. They believe anything they say, even if it is an obvious lie. However, once they realize that they are being deceived, they will walk away for good.

Things an ISFP May Lie About

ISFPs are sensitive individuals. When someone hurts their feelings, they smile and pretend that it doesn't bother them. Even if you ask them if they are OK, they will lie and say they are fine. They don't like awkward situations or making a scene, so they will lie even when your words hurt them.

MBTI Types That Can't Be Deceived

ENTJ

It is almost impossible to lie or deceive an ENTJ. In fact, they can also find out if someone is lying to them.

Things an ENTJ May Lie About

ENTJs may not be entirely truthful with people outside their close circle of friends and family. In certain situations, with strangers or acquaintances, they may keep certain details to themselves. They don't have bad intentions or want to be dishonest, but they care about their privacy, especially when it comes to sharing their feelings.

INTP

INTPs don't trust people easily, and they are very skeptical. If you tell them something or give them a piece of information, they will analyze it and do their research to ensure it is true.

Things an INTP May Lie About

INTPs often see the big picture and all the possibilities that can come with it. When it comes to challenges, they often ignore them. As a result, they may make false promises or sell people an idea before they have all the facts. They aren't exactly lying, but they usually miscalculate things. This is the result of their all-or-nothing attitude, which makes them go around promising people the world.

There are usually two sides to each personality type. Some people with the same personality type may lie for their own benefit, while others may lie to spare others' feelings. There are others that are simply incapable of lying. The information we have provided here can give you an idea of what each personality type may lie about. However, there are other things you need to look out for that you will learn about in the next chapters.

Chapter 7: Identifying Deception in People

The relationship between non-verbal communication and deception continues to attract much interest. In fact, research today suggests you cannot effectively detect deception in others through their non-verbal cues of communication. Meaning it is not scientifically a proven method of lie detection. Instead, it is a social science. As a field of study, social science examines society, people, and their behavior in the world around them.

The study of social science can help us understand how our own society works through social phenomena beyond our immediate experience. During the last several decades, extensive research literature has been published on lie detection and deceit in the fields of law and psychology. Many people are interested in lie detection for good reasons. Every day we lie, some of us more prolifically than others. We lie in our professional and personal relationships, and politicians and other public figures have a long history of lying in public.

Even though the scholarly community has rejected non-verbal cues as an effective way to detect deception, different law enforcement sectors, such as the CIA and FBI, still rely on it. Not to mention poker players, who are known to analyze their opponent's verbal cues to spot their bluffs. Identifying deception in people is difficult. The fact is, even though we see it every day, most people are not aware of exactly how much others are lying to them.

Why Is Identifying Deception in People Necessary?

Why do we place so much emphasis on the ability to detect lies through body language? There is increasing interest in deception detection techniques due to the fact that nonverbal communication is a significant social phenomenon.

No matter how you feel, have you ever kept your anger in check, expressed joy, or hidden your surprise? Nonverbal signals can be challenging to ignore or manipulate in professions where unconscious deception is not involved. Despite our conscious decision not to communicate verbally, our non-verbal communication always conveys meaning to others. Grumpy teenagers who don't communicate verbally with their parents will still send a message with a blank stare and a motionless stance.

The Credibility of Non-Verbal Communication

Despite the fact that verbal communication can sometimes fill in gaps left by non-verbal expressions, we often trust what people do more than what they say. As we face stress and danger, our behavior becomes instinctive, and we become more reliant on pre-evolution ways of thinking and acting. Non-verbal communication is sometimes involuntary and often subconscious; this innateness creates intuitive feelings about its genuineness. Blind children, who display similar facial expressions as others despite being blind since birth, illustrate the innateness of nonverbal signals. Essentially, it is less easy to fake non-verbal communication due to its involuntary or subconscious nature.

Nonverbal Cues and Deception

Each and every one of us has the ability to lie at some point in our lives. A number of studies have found that the average American tells between one and two lies a day. In spite of this, experts say that several non-verbal cues can be used to identify the person who is deceiving you.

Establish a Baseline

To analyze a person's body language, you must be aware of their usual body language. This is achieved through a method known as baselining. Handshakes and standing communicate a great deal about a person. You can identify someone's deception signals by identifying their baseline indicators first.

People can behave uncharacteristically for various reasons, not all of which suggest deception. However, don't be afraid to let loose your investigative side by observing how a person's conduct deviates from their baseline.

Examples of Baselining

You should know if a person is right-handed or left-handed if you know them well. A person who gestures or emphasizes statements with their non-dominant hand could be lying. Despite our minds' desire for honesty, the words we speak are what others hear. Our bodies can ultimately reveal deception.

One of the most famous examples of this is Bill Clinton. As a means of firmly expressing how he felt about Monica Lewinsky, he held up his right hand and arm forcefully and said, "I wasn't in a sexual relationship with her." It might have sounded credible, but the hand he used was not his dominant one.

We all have a baseline of what is considered normal for us. Fidgeting and continuously altering clothing are common behaviors for some people. To detect the baseline changes of this normal behavior, look for switches when attempting to identify deception.

However, these signals aren't fully reliable because if someone is uncomfortable in their seat, they might fidget; if someone is nervous, their voice might crack. Nonetheless, body language experts recommend paying attention to a few signals. Unfortunately, there is no magic trick that can tell you when someone is lying, but you can come pretty close by observing certain body language clues.

Examine Body Language

Itching, fidgeting, rocking movement, cocking the head to one side, or shuffling feet can indicate deception. A person's nervous system changes under stress, which can cause their body to tingle and feel itchy.

R. Edward Geiselman, a UCLA psychologist, found that dishonest people groom their hair when they engage in deceptive behavior.

What Do Their Hands Do?

It is more common for liars to display overt body language after speaking instead of prior to or during conversations. As the mind constructs stories, decides if they are credible, and makes changes, too much is happening.

University of Michigan researchers analyzed 120 video recordings from high-profile legal proceedings to investigate how individuals behave when telling the truth and lying. It is more common for those who lie to gesture widely compared to people who tell the truth. They discovered that people gestured 25% of the time when they were being truthful but 40% of the time when they were lying.

It is also common for deceitful people to hide their palms when lying, concealing information, or hiding their feelings. They may even tuck their hands in their pockets or tuck them out of view.

Watch Facial Expressions

Facial expressions play a role in non-verbal communication.
https://www.pexels.com/photo/woman-wearing-pink-top-1036620/

The face plays a key role in non-verbal communication. The face conveys so much information and emotion. Since the brain reacts to the world in two ways, relaxation and tension are two things to notice in the face. Let's start with comfort from a psychological perspective. When we smile or laugh, the pupils expand. Psychological distress typically appears in several areas simultaneously. People will furrow their foreheads, squint or tuck their chin to their chest. When someone is emotionally charged, their chin may vibrate as well. Covering the eyes can also be a sign of psychological discomfort. In other words, our non-verbal gestures instantly convey our emotions. How comfortable or uncomfortable is that behavior seem?

Change in Complexity

Do you ever notice that people go pale when they speak? It may be a clue to deceit when the blood drains from the face.

Dryness or Sweating

Because of alterations in the nervous system, liars can perspire, squint or blink excessively, have a dry mouth and eyes, over-swallow, or lick their lips.

Pay Attention to Their Tone and Sentence Structure

During times of stress, the muscles in people's vocal cords tighten, resulting in a high-pitched voice. Someone's voice may also crack. Clearing the throat is not only helpful for releasing tension but also for signaling deceit.

Volume change

Those who lie usually have louder voices. When we are defensive, we tend to speak louder.

How They Use Words

Some people may overcompensate by trying to persuade you that they are truthful by using terms such as "honestly," "let me be honest with you," etc. Filler words such as "uh," "like," and "um" are common indicators of deception, according to research conducted at the University of Michigan. These words are used more frequently by people attempting to buy time before saying something.

Inadvertent Errors

The majority of us are not born liars. Sometimes we speak the truth without realizing it. Someone might be lying if they say, "I was out with So-and-So - no, I was working late," or "I was fired - no, wait, I meant I quit."

Examine Their Eyes and Mouth

When someone purses their lips, it could be a sign that someone is suppressing their facts or feelings. Researchers at UCLA discovered that people who lie purse their lips after being confronted with difficult questions. Basically, it's an instinctive reaction that indicates a person does not want to speak.

The Eyes

If someone is lying, they may avoid eye contact or hold their gaze during a significant moment, indicating that they are contemplating their response. Blink rates can also reveal more about a person than you think.

Our blink rate can decrease when we are mentally stimulated. Still, it may increase when we are trying to come up with a storyline or when we are becoming increasingly anxious.

Despite that, the blink rate is not necessarily conclusive. It could signify that a person is lying if there is a clear shift from their baseline behavior.

Listen to How They Talk

Based on the fight or flight response, the concept of *cognitive complexity* is that when people lie, they tend to keep it as simple as possible. They will also typically only talk about two senses: what they hear and what they see. They don't necessarily add how things smelled, mention any spatial awareness, or talk about relationships or interactions with other people. They typically keep the conversation on a very shallow level. For example, consider the layers of an onion. When deceiving, liars will operate on the surface, first-level comprehension, where they were that day, and maybe who they were with. But when they get into the specifics and ask them questions about what they did during that time, what they were watching on TV, who won the football game, and who scored the last touchdown, their responses typically fall apart.

Their Attempt to Prove Their Honesty Might Be a Cover Up

To prove their innocence or honesty, someone involved in deception may try to convey their message in a manner that they think the other person wants to hear. The person may attempt to make it look as though they are not being dishonest if they are aware that you might think they are lying. So, they'll be very still when they're telling lies to not give anything away. Consider their baseline behavior when determining if this assessment is correct. For example, they may be fidgety, then go still during questioning. The stillness, then, is an indicator that they're being deceptive.

They Might Have Rehearsed All the Answers

When looking at non-verbal cues to indicate deception, it's helpful to concentrate on speech. Indicators of deception can include words such as "like" and "sort of," for example. When words like these are interjected in a sentence, it shows that the teller doesn't even have confidence in their story. For example, "I sort of did my homework" or "I kinda started to go to the gym." This kind of speech indicates that someone didn't finish the activity they claimed to have done. This means that they don't have the full story because they didn't actually do the thing they said they did.

Levels of Deception

There is perhaps no better way to classify lies than *by the people who tell them*.

Everyone has a tell - something that gives them away (like at the poker table). Friends, coworkers, family members, partners, and bosses may actually be concealing their true intentions under clever disguises. By recognizing and coping with liars, we can reduce the turmoil caused by them. Understanding the character traits of dishonest people will help us avoid being duped. In practice, this will make using the above tactics easier.

Deception can be classified into categories, each requiring a unique approach to identify or combat. Even though you can minimize the damage caused by a liar and reduce its effect, a liar cannot be changed. Honesty can help you reduce the negative effects of deception.

Average

Individuals in this category may say anything that maintains their self-esteem or keeps the conversation moving. Dishonest people often lie out of habit and have inconsistencies because they are not careful. A defiant person generally behaves in this way. More red flags are associated with this type of deceit than the examples listed below. They may find it tempting to continue lying when they start covering up some facts or altering the intensity of relevant information once they start doing so since it benefits them.

Slightly Above Average

This type of deception is a form of compulsive lying. Many of the things they say are questionable. If you don't know someone well, it can be challenging to deal with them. It's impossible to know what's going on without knowing their baseline behavior. In time, it becomes clear, however, that the person you now know is not the person you thought they were. When their professed values and actions don't match, it's hard to trust their word ever again.

Above Average

A person with a personality disorder is more likely to fall into this category. An imbalance in viewing reality is a hallmark of personality disorders such as borderline, narcissism, paranoia, histrionics, and obsessive-compulsive disorder. By telling lies, these personality types refuse to accept accountability. They are driven by their ego, which they defend no matter what.

Childish, abnormal behaviors are also common among above-average deceptive types, such as blaming others or inventing improbable accidents. Therefore, they can lead to resentment, annoyance, and suspicion if they are placed in authority. Due to their self-denial and unstable sense of self, they are unable to exercise morality or contemplation.

Advanced

Sociopaths and psychopaths will usually fall into this category of deception. According to research using computer-assisted brain scanning, the physical brain of these types of people differs from the brain of a person with a conscience. Liars with advanced pathologies have a hereditary component as well as a lack of nurture (neglect) from childhood. Stimuli activate normal human brains in response to empathy, responsibility, and moral conscience, but sociopathic and psychopathic brains are not.

These types of liars are the most damaging because they regularly lie without thinking or conscience. Since they have likely practiced duplicity on people their whole lives, these deceivers are very skilled. Society's rules and restrictions against lying have no meaning to them. As a tool for whatever exploit they wish to carry out, they can lie to you simply to satisfy their own needs since they lack respect for the truth and for others.

It is in their interests to cause confusion, uncertainty, and anger in others because they are not within society's norms of honesty. They are often highly functioning yet lie so pathologically that they don't even remember when they began deceiving others. Some may mess with people purely because it is fun. At the same time, others may deceive others to gain an advantage over them – rather than just deceiving them *all the time*.

Advanced personality types cannot comprehend rational arguments that contradict their agendas since their deceptions create conflict and uncertainty. They are to be avoided at all costs. When confronting those advanced in duplicity, experts recommend humility, rational agency, and honesty.

The issues of morality make deception particularly objectionable because it defies logic and human nature. More and more people are becoming aware of the importance of body language for communication and/or deception. For example, it is undisputed that the body language of a liar is often indicative of their feelings and thoughts. The more powerful the individual is, the more likely their behavior will be skewed by insecurity, even with their closest family members.

There are various ways to lie, from outright lying and full-on evasions to telling small white lies and making small inaccuracies. All of these are considered lies, which means that the person being deceived probably didn't know them to begin with. Some people may lie when they don't have anything to gain by doing so. Others may lie for the fun of it.

The study of deception is an in-depth science that has a lot to teach us about social interactions and the human condition. The goal is to try and understand how people lie, misperceive each other, and come to a consensus about the truth.

Chapter 8: Truth Indicators in Lies

Chances are that you've wondered if someone is lying to you at least a couple of times in your life. This feeling can be very disappointing, especially when the one in question is a loved one.

According to a recent study, most of our day-to-day communications are honest, provided that you're not dealing with a prolific liar. This study spanned 632 participants and lasted for around 91 days. This experiment required all participants to log the lies they told daily on an online survey. A total of 116366 lies were observed over this period. However, it was found that around 75% of the sampled individuals didn't tell many lies. They averaged 0 to 2 lies a day. Additionally, most of these lies were insignificant or white lies, such as complimenting a friend who asked if they looked too horrible on one of their bad days. That said, around 6% of the participants who also told relatively few lies had days where they exhibited higher numbers of lies.

This survey is particularly unique because this study spanned a longer time period instead of collecting responses from a certain sample via a one-time survey. This allowed researchers to notice and examine changes in behavior. It was found that each person's lying tendencies differ from day to day. Even generally honest individuals tell lies at times. Similarly, prolific liars don't always hesitate to tell the truth. All in all, prolific liars were the ones who varied in their lying tendencies the most; this variation was particularly prominent among the top 1% of all liars. These individuals told an average of 17 lies a day. On the other hand, the top 1% of the most honest individuals exhibited the least variation in their truth-telling habits.

Before we delve deeper into how you can detect lies and unravel the truth, it helps to learn some statistics about lies. This can give you insight into how often people lie, the types of lies they tell, the most common reasons behind them, and who they lie to the most.

Statistics about Lies

The same study also explored the reasons behind the lies that people tell. The highest percentage of lies, 21%, were told in an effort to avoid others. 20%, the following percentage, is often told for the purpose of jokes and pranks. 14% of lies are told for the sake of self-protection, and 13% are told to appear more impressive. 11% of the lies that people tell are for the purpose of protecting others, 9% of the lies told are for personal gain, and 5% are told to benefit another person. 2% of the lies that people tell are aimed at hurting another person, and the last 5% of lies are told either for no reason or for unspecified purposes.

According to the survey, 75% of the participants told 0 to 2 lies a day. Lies appeared to make up 7% of these individuals' communications. 90% of their lives were insignificant or white lies. It was found that 51% of the lies told were directed at friends, 21% were told to family members, 11% of lies were told to schoolmates and work colleagues, 8.9% of lies were directed at strangers, and 8.5% were told to casual connections.

The survey, as we mentioned above, reveals that most lies people tell are little white lies. The report referred to 88.6% of all the lies said as "little white lies." The other 11.4% were considered to be big and significant lies.

Now that you have a general picture of the nature of people's lives, you are ready to take action. In this chapter, you'll understand how to unearth truths that are hidden with lies. You'll come across a list that covers the indicators of truth.

How to Tell When Someone Is Lying to You

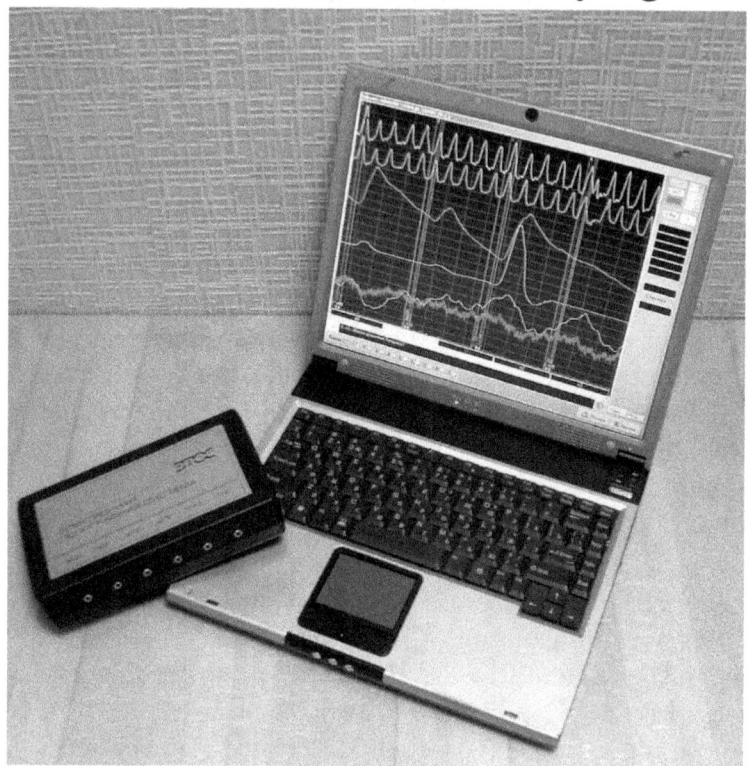

Polygraphs can help you determine if someone is lying to you.
https://commons.wikimedia.org/wiki/File:Polygraph1.jpg

When it comes to lies, manipulation, and deception, referring to psychology would be your best bet. Understanding the way that a person's thoughts and feelings affect their behavior can help you get a good idea of the dynamics of the lie at hand. Only then will you be able to unearth the truth. While having a polygraph would save you trouble and heartache, getting hold of one is not always possible. Fortunately, some behavioral signs can help point you in the right direction that you can look out for. It's important to note that even though these clues are generally very helpful, they are still not entirely accurate. Science and psychology still haven't reached a surefire method that can help you spot if someone is lying right away. That said, a recent notable test seems to have great potential for success. This test, which is known as the Psychologically Based Credibility Assessment Tool, or PBCAT, was developed in 2013 by Jacqueline Evans, a psychologist at the University of Texas at Tyler, and her partners. This assessment scale is based on an 11-item rating scale. This scale can be tweaked to suit the purpose at hand.

Psychologically Based Credibility Assessment Tool

A sample of 46 college students, who were predominantly females and Hispanics, was selected to aid in the development of the PBCAT. These students were asked to watch videos of a target student in which they spoke about what they had done on the previous Saturday night within a specified timeframe. The target students were truthful in some of the videos and lied in others. Whether they lied or told the truth, the target students were also asked to explain what they had done in either a backward or forward-going chronology.

The main idea behind asking some of the participants to tell the order of events in backward chronology is that it required more mental effort. As you are probably aware, telling a story in reverse order of events is much harder than telling it orderly. Overworking a person's mental capacity is known as cognitive load. This stimulates a similar mental state as the one you would experience in high-pressure situations, such as being called in as a witness at the police station, explaining to the insurance agent how your accident occurred, or attending a job interview. In those cases, there are a lot of risks, which could lead to either a positive or negative outcome attached to the truth or lies you tell.

Lying is more mentally taxing than telling the truth. This is because, when devising a lie, you have to be very careful when it comes to the context. Everything we do is driven by several situations and triggers a series of outcomes even when we don't realize it.

Let's say you have two close friends. You ask one of them, X, to tag along on a certain errand, totally forgetting to tell your other friend, Y, as well. Later at night, Y texts to check in on you and asks how your day went. You tell them that you went to pick something up at the mall, but you don't mention that X tagged along because it might hurt their feelings. They ask you if you've spoken to X recently, and you tell them that you haven't because you feel slightly panicked. There's a moment of awkward silence before they say, "how come? X told me that they asked for your opinion on the shirt that they saw this morning." Words start rolling off your tongue in hopes of salvaging the situation. Y can already tell that something's not quite right.

In other words, lying requires you to get all your facts straight. You must also be careful when you're accounting for all the details. Once you go into the spiral that is lying, you need to accurately remember the facts you changed and beware of the additional lies you may have to come up with if more questions are asked. Say your partner asked you how much your new dress costs. You tell them that you got it for $100 when it really cost you $200. Later that night, a friend asks you where you bought your dress from when you were all hanging out. If the store you purchased the dress from is known for being a bit pricey, you'll tell your friend that you got it at a different store. This way, you can stay consistent with the first lie you told. When you get back home, you'll probably need to get rid of the shopping bag and cut the tags off your dress, so your partner doesn't stumble across the truth. If you go to the mall together, you may have to go the extra mile to avoid passing by either store.

Let's go back to the PBCAT experiment. The individuals who were supposed to decide whether their peers were lying or telling the truth were taught basic PBCAT methods. They took the time to reflect on the facts and whether they added up. You probably guessed it; participants could detect lies more effectively when the person in the video explained how they spent their afternoon in backward chronological order.

There was also another variation of this study. Researchers assigned cognitive load to the participant's English fluency rather than their ability to recall events in reverse chronological order. Naturally, native English speakers experienced the least mental pressure. Non-native but fluent or highly proficient English speakers experienced slightly additional cognitive load. Finally, English speakers with low proficiency levels were under the most cognitive load. Lying in a second language is a lot more difficult than lying in your mother tongue.

The PBCAT proved to be an effective method of detecting lies and deception when used in this variant of the experiment, as well. The targets with the highest mental pressure and cognitive load levels were the most obvious liars. If you think about it, police interrogation rooms are designed to create a cognitive load so suspects would be more likely to confess to their crimes. The layout of the room is intended to increase stress and anxiety levels, making the suspect feel isolated and uncomfortable.

The 9 Basic PBCAT Rating Scales

Now that you understand what the PBCAT is and the theory behind it, you can now use the following 9 basic rating scales that will help you determine if someone is lying:

1. The elimination of sensory details. Genuine and honest people often include details regarding their thoughts and feelings. For instance, if your friend is telling you about the time when they won a race, they may say things like, "all I remember thinking at that moment was how close I was to the finish line," or "my heart felt like it was going to burst when they awarded me the medal." They may also mention other details, such as the music that played in the background or the runner-up's score. Since these details are harder to make up and stay consistent with, liars often eliminate them together later.

2. They constantly claim that they have a weak memory. It's not that hard to remember the dynamics of a situation or event if you've experienced it first-hand. Everyone forgets irrelevant bits and pieces. However, you will likely remember the general flow of events if you've lived through a certain situation. Since they've probably had to tell several renditions of the same story, expanding on the lie every time they speak of it, they lose sight of the initial story they told. This is why it's a lot easier for them to claim to have a weak memory to excuse their tendency to mess up certain details.

3. They make unnecessary fixes. As we mentioned above, liars come up with numerous renditions of their stories. Since they go back and forth so much, they make unnecessary and heavy fixes to their stories. They may throw numerous names around or correct the location they mentioned multiple times. We all make mistakes sometimes; therefore, there isn't a specific number of faults you should look out for. However, you should know that something isn't right if these corrections happen frequently enough for you to notice them.

4. They don't bother to get into the details. If someone tells you a long, elaborate, and detailed story, then chances are that this is what really happened. As we have already explained above, liars don't want to risk falling into the trap of messing things up. Since

their lives are formulated inside their minds, they have no core memory to recall back to. We're more prone to forgetting things that we've never experienced. This is why they will not put in the time and effort to develop a long-form, detailed lie that they may forget later.

5. They make contradictory and irrational statements. Your ears shouldn't be the only tool you use to detect the authenticity of the story. You also need to use your other senses and what you know. The truth will hold up much better than one lie followed by another. Remember the example of the dress that we mentioned above? Imagine you're asking your friend where she bought her dress from. If the dress looks expensive, then it's probably from a better-quality store than the one she mentioned. If you're into fashion, you'd probably be able to tell if the dress's style and finish are similar to the garments you'd see in the store that she mentioned. If what your eye sees doesn't align with the other person's words, then they're probably lying. This tip is particularly useful in situations or topics that you're well-versed in.

6. They take the time to ponder deeply. You'd be able to tell if the person you're speaking to is confident in their ability to recall the story. If they feel hesitant or seem to be putting a lot of time and effort into answering your questions or coming up with a reasonable continuation to their story, this is a sign that they're experiencing cognitive load. Everyone may struggle to remember certain events. However, if the situation was recent or significant, they shouldn't be pondering every word that rolls off their tongue. For instance, if you ask your partner why their ex contacted them a couple of days ago, they should be able to tell you what happened without pausing to think every other sentence.

7. You can tell that they're tense, anxious, and nervous. Only great and experienced liars can go through a series of lies without getting even a little anxious. One of the signs that an individual might be a psychopath is that they're able to tell a string of lies without feeling even a bit of discomfort. As long as they're not telling a painful story, honest individuals should be able to tell a story while feeling relaxed or at least comfortable.

8. They'll be unusually positive. When someone tries to impress others, or at least leave a positive impression on them, they want to

be as positive as possible. If they try to come off as cool and unbothered in situations where others would normally make a few complaints, then they're likely trying to deceive you. They may try to hide their negative reactions and behaviors in an effort to get you to like them.

9. They are very slow talkers. When people tell the truth, they talk at a normal, reasonable pace. Those who lie, however, will take more time to formulate sentences. This is because they're trying to be consistent, positive, and believable. Most people think that liars are fast talkers. Besides the fact that anxiety may cause you to talk faster than usual, fast-talking liars, such as salespeople, for instance, are just trying to confuse you. Their lies are also well-rehearsed and memorized. However, when someone is caught red-handed, they will take their time to come up with a seamless, well-thought-out tale. They need to improvise, with caution, of course, as they go.

Unearthing the Truth from a Lie

More often than not, liars mess up and even give themselves away when they get caught up in a long string of lies. The more elaborate and complex the lie, the more likely the truth is hidden within. Many liars also tell half-truths. Instead of formulating an entire story with nothing but their imagination, it's easier for them to reveal actual details they don't mind sharing and replace the things they would like to keep hidden with stories of their choice. Since not everyone is trained to pick up on verbal and behavioral cues, the truth still goes unnoticed. The following list includes some signs that a person is telling the truth:

- Their story is long and conveys emotions and sensory details
- They are able to maintain reasonable or adequate amounts of eye contact throughout the story
- They are not fidgety, and their breathing isn't shaky. They feel comfortable
- Their tone of voice is generally steady
- They don't try to blame others for their shortcomings
- They're not trying too hard to keep a positive impression
- They're not blinking at a faster or slower-than-usual rate

- They're not intentionally covering their throat for no apparent reason
- They're not playing around with their hair or accessories, nor do they keep touching their nose
- Their sentences are complete and coherent. They don't pose unnecessarily between words or phrases

If you know that someone is lying but returns to a calmer and more neutral state every now and then throughout the story, then know that these periods of comfort are when they tell the truth.

Learning the 9 basic PBCAT rating scales can help you understand which areas to work on if you wish to lie. Avid liars are always insistent on improving their ability to tell seamless lies. If you don't have ill intentions, then this credibility assessment tool can easily help you catch liars. Ideally, you should aim to get your target person to tell the story in question from scratch. You are more likely to catch onto a person's lies and pinpoint the truth when they're the ones telling the story. If you ask them questions instead, they'll have the time to come up with straightforward and convincing answers.

Chapter 9: How to Read People like a Book

This chapter focuses on everything you need to know to read people like a book. It serves as a summary of many previous chapters, mainly focusing on how to understand verbal cues and read non-verbal cues. It also includes information on the different personality types. It offers all the tools you need to pick up on what a person is feeling and thinking right away. You will also come across a step-by-step guide on all the things you need to pay attention to when you're trying to read a person.

Understanding Verbal Cues

If you're a generally sensitive person, then you are probably aware that a person's tone of voice is one of the cornerstones of communication. Empaths and sensitive people can easily point out changes in a person's way of communication. Even if a person is nice and friendly, sensitive individuals may spend a lot of time working out what the slightly rougher overtone in that person's voice means.

The message behind our choice of words can differ drastically, depending on our tone of voice. This is why, for instance, it's very hard to pick up on sarcastic remarks over text. If you think about it, texting often results in many misunderstandings because it lacks the emotion and the room for expression that comes with verbal or tonal communication. Think of all the times you wrote a text and didn't hit "send" because you thought it was better to talk to them over the phone or in person.

Everything about how our voices sound, including their volume, clarity, timbre, and speed of talking, impacts the message we're trying to communicate.

Try turning on a random foreign-language movie and watching a random scene. Keep the subtitles off and listen. Even if you don't understand what the characters are saying, chances are you would be able to tell how they feel and even gather a little insight into what they're thinking just by listening to their tone of voice.

The Tone of Voice and the Perception of Others

If someone has a deep tone of voice, then you're likely to perceive them as mature. They give off the feeling that they can be trusted, which is why many organizations use this tone in their TV, video, and radio advertisements. An extremely deep tone, however, can be a little unsettling.

Individuals who speak in a steady, confident tone of voice can make you feel like they're highly accomplished or important in their community. Similarly, a quiet or shy tone communicates that the speaker is weak, insecure, or feels rather awkward. As counter-intuitive as it sounds, people who speak in a very high tone of voice are thought to be less credible than others. You can tell a lot about a person's identity and what they wish to communicate about themselves just by paying attention to their tone of voice. A person's tone of voice is also used as evidence in trials, holding the same reliability as fingerprints.

Speed of Breathing and Pace of Life

If you pay attention to someone's breathing speed, you can gain insight into their pace in life. A calm breathing speed suggests that the individual is generally balanced and attuned to their surroundings. Energetic and active people usually breathe deeply and consistently. Angry individuals take deep and strong breaths. Someone with slight or superficial breaths isn't very practical in life. Finally, short and rapid breaths suggest that the speaker feels anxious, in pain, or uncomfortable.

The Volume of Voice and Ability to Interact

When someone speaks at a normal volume, this reveals that the person has self-control. They can listen to what others have to say. High volumes, however, hint at a weakness in the speaker's personality. They also suggest that they're highly impatient and even selfish. A low speaking volume can give you the impression that someone is shy and inexperienced.

Vocalization and the Sense of Being Understood

Vocalization is directly associated with a person's need and ability to be understood by those around them. When someone's articulation is clear and defined, this shows that they are open to interacting with others. It also gives a good impression of their mental state and clarity. Imprecise articulation typically corresponds to deceptive individuals. It may also hint at a state of mental chaos or confusion. When someone is able to very clearly articulate their words, they are perceived as narcissistic. Very clear vocalization is also linked to tension. If someone stumbles over their words, then they're either shy or aggressive.

Speed of Talking and Emotional State

You can tell a lot about a person's emotional health by observing their talking speed. If someone usually speaks very slowly, they probably feel disconnected and disinterested in the world around them. A regular talking speed may suggest that the person is holding something back. They may even be bottling up their emotions. When speaking quickly, the person is usually trying to hide something. A rapid talking speed may also suggest that there's tension. Varying or irregular speeds reveal that the person is anxious or confused.

The Tone of Voice and Your Relationship

Listening to a person's tone of voice can help you understand where you stand or your relationship with them. It can also give your insight into their boundaries. If someone has a sharp and cold tone of voice, then they wish to create some distance between you. They wish to get closer to you if they're talking in a warm and friendly tone. Think of a person's tone of voice as an indicator of your bond. While some elements of a person's tone remain consistent, the overall essence can change. This depends on their mood, energy levels, and more.

Reading Non-Verbal Cues

Reading non-verbal cues can be quite challenging at first. However, the more you practice it, the more naturally it will come to you. Picking up on non-verbal cues is essential when it comes to effective communication. It can help you significantly in your personal and professional life. Even though some non-verbal cues are unique to each person, there are some common signals that you can learn. This will help you learn a lot about other people's intentions, desires, drives, motivations, and emotions. You may be surprised to learn that most of what people try to communicate doesn't solely depend on their words. Around 70% of our communications rely on non-verbal cues. This is why it's important to be mindful of a person's choice of words, tone of voice, and the following non-verbal cues.

What Their Posture Says

By observing a person's posture, you can tell if a person is fully present in your conversation. If their back is straight and their shoulders are pushed slightly backward, then this is a sign that they're actively listening to what you have to say. They are engaged in the conversation and are open to your thoughts and ideas. A poor or slouched posture or tensed shoulder muscles communicate that the person you're talking to is uncomfortable. They may be angry, distressed, anxious, or nervous.

How They Use Their Arms

Crossed arms suggest negative feelings.
https://www.pexels.com/photo/a-sad-woman-standing-at-the-kitchen-area-8929453/

If you want to get an idea of how a person feels throughout your conversation, make sure to keep track of how they use their arms. Someone who keeps them down to their side or allows them to rest on the table shows that they're rather optimistic. Open arms could also suggest that they're open to receiving new information. Keeping their arms closed, such as crossing them over their chest, suggests negative feelings.

Notice Their Legs

If someone rests both feet flat on the ground, this could suggest the same as keeping open arms, that is, active listening and being open to ideas. Crossing one's legs or keeping them closed suggests annoyance or stress.

Be Mindful of Facial Expressions

It comes as no surprise that facial expressions such as furrowed eyebrows, pursed lips, a scowl, or a frown are not good signs. Take a moment to check if the person you're talking to is angry or confused. On the other hand, a gentle smile, relaxed facial muscles, or even a slightly raised eyebrow are all positive signs that the listener is engaged.

Learning about Different Personality Types

Learning about different personality types and understanding the differences between them can help you learn more about yourself and those around you. You will understand different people's preferences and learn all about their motives. Understanding the various personality types can help you determine how you can lead others, express yourself, and communicate with people. It can also help you collaborate and work with those around you, as well as negotiate and reach reasonable compromises. Understanding different personalities can serve as great stress management and problem-solving tool. When you know how to deal with each person, you will be able to build and maintain closer bonds with people, expand your social and professional network, and enhance your performance in the workplace. This skill is especially beneficial to managers because it can help them become better leaders, communicators, instructors, and decision-makers.

Personalities can be broken down into five main traits, conscientiousness, agreeableness, neuroticism, openness, and extroversion. These traits are typically arranged in either acronym: CANOE or OCEAN.

The first trait, **conscientiousness,** refers to individuals who tend to do their work in a responsible and thorough manner. They are often better academic performers and can easily find success in their careers.

Agreeable people, as you can tell from the name, are liked by others. They are great company and are easy to get along with.

Neurotic individuals are characterized by their mood swings and high anxiety levels. They are usually very sensitive and emotional.

The fourth trait, **openness,** refers to a person's openness to experiencing new things in life. These individuals are curious and adventurous. They are typically successful in several areas of life and are excellent creative thinkers.

The last trait, **extroversion**, corresponds to people who enjoy stimulation. They like to try things out, especially ones that they know would allow them to reap great rewards.

It's important to note that these traits are inherently good or bad. They just vary in different levels and tendencies from one person to another, depending on the way that they deal with the problems that they encounter in life. You need to consider two things when you're getting to know someone - understanding how their personality works and how they fit under the five traits we mentioned above and learning when and how to apply these labels. The first thing you need to know, however, is that there is no black and white when it comes to personalities. People are not always entirely conscientious or irresponsible, nor are they entirely introverted or extroverted. Many people lie in the middle of the spectrum of each of the traits above.

How to Apply the Big Five Traits

Se/Extroverted Sensing

These individuals thrive when they find themselves in a stimulating environment. They enjoy places that offer a range of sensory input. They don't perform best when they sit at a desk all day long. They enjoy professions where they can move around, attend meetings, talk to people, and tackle challenges.

Si/Introverted Sensing

As opposed to Se, those people prefer environments that aren't stimulating. They like to work by the book and prefer to follow instructions. They appreciate road maps, progress tracking, a to-do list, and constructive feedback.

Ni/Introverted Intuiting

Ni likes to take some time off from the pressures of the external world. They thrive whenever they are given the opportunity to self-reflect and activate their inner workings. When communicating with them or presenting an idea to them, it's always a good idea to offer sensory focus. For instance, if you're reading something to them, you can help them stay focused by showing them the text and using your finger as a guide. They like to visualize and explore the nitty-gritty details of new ideas.

Ne/Extroverted Intuiting

Those people like to be given a wide array of inputs when it comes to brainstorming. They think best when they're exposed to numerous distractions because this is how they get inspired. They don't necessarily follow a linear track when pursuing their goals. They are easily swayed. However, it's their way of making great things happen. They like to explore the relationships between various ideas, and they enjoy mind games.

Te/Extroverted Thinking

Extroverted thinkers are very economical when it comes to how they use their minds. Their focus automatically shifts to the things they can measure. They know which words to pick up on and the things that they need to pay attention to when making decisions. They don't like to waste their time by engaging in unimportant matters. They only use facts and respond to them. They prefer using informative visuals like grids, diagrams, maps, and charts. They are very competent at school and work.

Ti/Introverted Thinking

When making decisions, those individuals rely on inner and complex thought processes. The entire reasoning procedure happens inside their brain, meaning that they don't necessarily need to refer to any sensory inputs. They deduce information, categorize it, and even create a little pro and con chart inside their brain. This is why they like to make decisions on their own. They like to take their time to correct their mistakes as they are perfectionists. They aim for accuracy. Since they are introverts, social and emotional inputs can be very stressful for them.

Fe/Extroverted Feeling

Even though these individuals are very attentive to what you say and pay a close eye to what you're thinking of them, their physical appearance or reactions will never reveal that. They hold their ethics and personal beliefs in the highest regard. You may often find yourself discussing topics like justice and righteousness with them. When communicating with those people, it helps to pay more attention to your word choice than your tone of voice. Make sure to assign value to every word you speak. For instance, if you're upset with them, make sure to communicate this through your words and not through your tone.

Fi/Introverted Feeling

Unlike extroverted individuals, introverted people listen more to a person's tone of voice than to their choice of words. They care more about the motive behind the words you speak and pay attention to things you may have left unsaid. They listen to your values and beliefs. When communicating with those individuals, following the same concept is best. Speak to their beliefs while staying genuine and authentic to who you are.

How to Read People like a Book: A Step-By-Step Guide

Step 1: Set Realistic Expectations

To read someone like a book, you must be willing to put in the time and energy needed to understand them. You can't get a glimpse of the target person or spend a few minutes with them before you decide that you know everything about how they think and feel. Don't get discouraged even when it takes you more time than anticipated to truly understand someone. We are all products of lifetimes of experiences and complex, pent-up emotions.

Step 2: Let Go of All Your Assumptions

When meeting someone new, you may often get the feeling that you will never be able to understand or get along with them. Often, you'll get off on the wrong foot when meeting someone, and that's okay. It helps to treat everyone you meet as if they were a blank slate. Don't let their appearance or even first impression get the best of you. Remind yourself that you know nothing about that person until you make an effort to get to know them.

Step 3: Be Engaged and Present

You'll never be able to understand others as long as you're stuck in your own head. When talking to someone, direct all your focus and energy toward getting to know and understanding them. If you find it hard to step out of your head or quiet down your thoughts, practice different grounding and mindfulness techniques and implement one that works best for you. Take a deep breath and bring yourself back to the present moment.

Step 4: Capitalize on the Importance of Perspective

We all have different and unique perspectives on the same thing. When dealing with someone, remind yourself that their views are likely quite different from yours. Brace yourself for misunderstandings, and never let them be a setback. Practice viewing things from other people's perspectives while working on communicating your own views as clearly and calmly as possible. Try to figure out their personality type and express yourself accordingly.

Step 5: Pay Attention to Body Language

As mentioned above, non-verbal cues often speak much louder than words. When you're communicating with others, don't forget to watch out for the positions of their arms and legs, their ability to hold eye contact, and their facial expressions. Even the basics of body language can significantly help you in your communication efforts.

Step 6: Practice Active Listening

Unfortunately, technology has sneaked its way into all aspects of our lives. People everywhere can be seen scrolling through their phones while "conversing" with others. Even when they're not distracted by technology, they're consumed in their inner thoughts. Practice being an active listener and focus on what people are saying. Learn to understand the significance of their word choice and pick up on their tone of voice.

Step 7: Reflect on What They Say

Reflecting on what other people tell you by repeating their words as you understand them can help them warm up to you. It makes you appear more trustworthy and helps others feel comfortable around you.

Step 8: Don't Forget to Ask Questions

Avoid asking questions that start with "why," as this encourages them to question themselves. It leads to a forward and backward cycle, and it creates confusion. Learn to ask questions that start with "what" and "how" to keep them engaged.

Now that you have read this chapter, you should be able to understand people and read them easily. You can practice these methods on anyone, whether you've known them for a while or whether you're meeting them for the first time. While it can be tricky at first, analyzing people will get a lot easier and feel more natural over time.

Bonus: Analyzing People's Cheat Sheet

Understanding human behavior becomes pretty simple if we correlate body language and verbal and non-verbal cues with certain situations. While it's true that every human being is distinct and has a unique personality, these cues might even differ drastically for people. However, most humans have been wired to perform certain physical cues when faced with similar situations. Thus, analyzing people is not as difficult as you might imagine.

Non-verbal cues, particularly, can greatly convey how a person feels about a certain situation. And while people get better at hiding their true feelings with age, a trained observer can easily spot little quirks and traits that accompany certain feelings and emotions. Consequently, reading and analyzing someone's body language holds much more power than you can imagine. However, not everyone is trained in this field. You've already learned about various verbal and non-verbal cues and how to decode human behavior. As a bonus, this chapter will go into comprehensive detail about each body part and how varying body language and appearance can be used to identify a person's emotions and personality.

The Head and Forehead

Women ventilating their hair is associated with releasing stress and heat.
https://unsplash.com/photos/FXB1vh4oTek?utm_source=unsplash&utm_medium=referral&utm_content=creditShareLink

The head can be considered the most important part of the body as it houses the brain, through which all behavioral signals are generated. How a person adorns their head and the gestures associated with certain situations are key indicators of a person's emotions. When focusing on the head and forehead of a person, be sure to notice the following traits, quirks, and behaviors:

- Mostly observed in women when they casually play with their hair, in the sense that they stroke, twist, or twirl strands between fingers; this can have two indications. They're in a comfortable mood, or they're stressed. However, these emotions are almost opposite to each other, so how do you tell the difference? Well, it's simple: if a person is playing with their hair with their palm facing out, they're content, comfortable, and confident. Whereas, when they have their palm facing their head, this trait is more of a pacifying gesture, where the person in question feels stressed or uncomfortable.

- Ventilating hair, for both men and women, is considered a powerful pacifier associated with releasing stress and heat. Men usually run their hands through their hair to relieve heat or stress. Whereas women lift up the hair from the nape of their neck whenever they feel stressed, flustered, or worried.

- People, particularly women, are often seen pulling, flipping, or playing with their hair. This trait is often an unconscious one, done to attract the attention of a romantic interest. However, when this hair pulling is observed to be aggressive or repetitive, with a higher intensity than normal, it indicates high levels of stress.

- Head patting, scratching, and striking are usually observed when a person is faced with a dilemma or is conflicted about a stressful decision. These gestures are considered to be soothing and help pacify stress and anxiety.

- An obvious sign of stress on the forehead appears as a series of lines or stiffened muscles. Over time, these stiffened muscles result in deep grooves and indentations, more commonly known as stress lines. When observed in young people, they're indicators of a tough life filled with worry.

- If the temporal veins on a person's forehead seem to twitch or become overly visible, it indicates feelings of stress, anxiety, frustration, or even anger.

The Eyebrows

Our eyebrows have many purposes, but most importantly, they're used to convey our emotions. Facial expressions hold a powerful role in conveying one's feelings and emotions, and without the varying movements of the eyebrows, it would become very difficult to read what a person is trying to convey. For instance:

- When a person arches or flashes both their eyebrows at the same time, they indicate excitement, recognition, or happiness. This expression is one of the most positive gestures our eyebrows can make. In contrast, eyebrow arching is also done when a person is faced with a surprising situation. The difference here is that this gesture is a bit tense as compared to the former one. Moreover, it is usually held a few seconds longer than an appreciable eyebrow arch.

- Asymmetric eyebrow arches, on the other hand, indicate a questioning stance. One eyebrow arches high while the other one stays in the same position or moves lower.

Eyes

People often say eyes are windows to one's soul. What they really mean by this phrase is that eyes convey much more than any other body part can. In fact, it's one of the first things people notice about you. Eyes can indicate many emotions, including:

- While you might have associated pupil dilation and constriction with changes in light, it's actually very much affected by emotional changes in a person's mind. When a person is with someone they're comfortable with, someone they like, or love, their pupils tend to dilate to absorb as much light as possible. Whereas pupil constriction takes place when you see something unpleasant or negative. This could include both situations and/or people.

- Relaxed eyes are comfort indicators, conveying that a person is not tense. Whereas squinting or tense eyes signal that there's something bothering the person in question. This is because the muscles around our eyes are much more receptive to stressors as compared to other facial features and so can be easily observed to know when a person is stressed. Similarly, quivering around the eyes can be an indicator of underlying stress or anxiety.

- Apprehension, doubt, or concern will cause the orbits of a person's eyes to narrow, resulting in an overall narrowed point of sight.

- How frequently a person blinks is a good indicator of their emotions, depending on the situation and environment. While every person differs somewhat, blinking faster than their usual blink rate indicates that they are nervous or attracted to someone they're talking to. Moreover, rapid blinking sometimes also happens when people try to stop tears from rolling out of their eyes.

- While social and cultural norms govern eye contact, they also reflect a person's nature, confidence, and personality. Whether or not a person holds eye contact (and how long they hold it) tells a lot about someone's personality and intentions. Avoidance of eye contact is indicative of many things; however, contrary to popular belief, it is not indicative of deception. In contrast, people tend to avoid eye contact with people they find obnoxious, unpleasant, or repressive.

- Moreover, people who are more confident, and hold high status in society, tend to hold longer eye contact while speaking and listening. Whereas people with lower self-confidence or status tend to maintain eye contact while listening but not so much while speaking.
- Eye contact for longer periods of time can be classified into gazing and staring. Gazing is when someone looks lovingly at another person. Whereas staring indicates that a person is suspicious or confrontational, usually done to assert dominance. Staring for long periods of time is often offensive.
- Darting eyes back and forth is associated with processing information, particularly negative information, fear, or concern. While many people consider this quirk to be indicative of deception and lying behavior, it actually indicates that the person in question is considering their options or thinking of solutions.
- Glazed eyes are a sign of substance use. People under the influence of alcohol, marijuana, or any other kind of drug can have glazed or reddish eyes.
- When a person looks sideways in the middle of a conversation or when asked a question, it shows their reluctance to commit to something, disregard for something, or contempt.

Ears

Our ears communicate in ways we could never imagine, and they give rise to a number of quirks and gestures that reflect our emotions. These may include:

- Turning one's ears towards the speaker indicates that we are listening intently or trying to listen more closely to what they are saying. It conveys that we consider what the other person is trying to say to be important.
- Ears turning pink or a shade of red indicates the body's reaction to a range of emotions. For instance, it could be due to anger, embarrassment, frustration, nervousness, or arousal.
- When a person pulls on their earlobe or slightly massages it, they are either contemplating something, hesitating, or considering their options.

Nose and Lips

Playing with the nose is an essential part of forming the overall facial expression that conveys our feelings and emotions. Without these two features, our faces would be a bit bland, and a lot of communication through non-verbal cues would be misinterpreted. These cues usually include:

- Scrunching or wrinkling the nose upward, both symmetrically and unilaterally, reflects feelings of disgust, displeasure, dislike, or something.
- The slight twitching of the nose suggests a linguistic shortcut that could mean different things in different cultures – but most commonly refers to a wordless question.
- Brushing one's nose repeatedly indicates stress or psychological discomfort. This is, again, a pacifying gesture meant to bring down stress levels.
- People who hold their noses high, with their chin tilted slightly upwards, tend to be more confident. This could also be indicative of arrogance, feelings of superiority, and even indignation.
- Nostril flares usually signal preparation for getting into a physical altercation. People tend to flare their nostrils when they are getting ready to act out violently.
- People purse their lips when stressed and leave them full when content and comfortable. Lip fullness can thus be indicative of a person's emotional state.
- Lip pulling or plucking is often associated with low confidence, stress, fear, or other problems a person might be facing. If someone does this continually, it is likely a pacifier and doesn't reflect a problem. However, people who don't often show this behavior may have a serious issue they're dealing with.
- Similarly, lip biting and licking are generally done for the same reasons as above. Continually licking one's lips, particularly, is a reliable indicator of one being very stressed.

Chin, Cheeks, and Jaw

While many would argue that the cheeks, jaw, and chin were dormant features and couldn't in any way contribute to our body language, they couldn't be more wrong. Sudden facial tics can often indicate changes in emotions with regard to varying situations. These can include:

- Facial tics often happen near the cheeks, usually due to a nervous twitch or anxiousness.
- Cheek strumming indicates boredom and a person wanting to move on from the situation or conversation. Cheek framing is done to aid in concentration or focus on something more intensely.
- When people are under a lot of stress, they tend to swipe across their cheeks in a downward motion as a way to relieve stress. This gesture is usually considered a pacifier.
- Tightening of the jaw muscles usually indicates anger, stress, frustration, or other negative emotions. The jaw is jutted out, particularly when a person is angry.
- Anxiousness or excessive worry leads to chin withdrawal, where people unconsciously bring their chin towards their necks to protect their vitals. Whereas chin drops indicate that a person has given up or lost hope.
- Chin touching is observed when a person is in thought about something, but it can also be a sign of doubt or fear.
- A very famous pose or body language is the chin-to-shoulder posture. This is usually observed when people feel embarrassed or are emotionally vulnerable.

The Neck

The neck is considered to be the most vulnerable part of the body. Thus, gestures and cues associated with it often have something to do with protective gestures and unconscious actions. These cues include:

- Neck touching is usually associated with insecurity and anxiousness. People frequently touching their necks can be a sign that they're going through some trouble and that they may need help.

- Both men and women tend to cover the neck dimple, located below Adam's apple and just above the chest. This is considered the weakest part of the body, and thus, we tend to cover this region whenever we feel threatened. This behavior can be explained as an evolutionary reaction as a result of shielding from acts of predation or aggression.
- People often have a hand massaging the side of their necks, which is where the vagus nerve is located. This gesture acts as a pacifier because stimulation of the vagus nerve results in the heart rate going down. So, people subconsciously do this to relieve stress and anxiety.
- People tend to swallow hard when they're either stressed, scared, or frustrated. This makes the muscles around their throat tighten, resulting in difficulty swallowing.
- Neck exposure, in contrast to the neck covering cue, is one of the most disarming gestures one can do. Something about making yourself vulnerable to the other person is so remarkable that it instantly wins over anyone.

Shoulders, Arms, and Hands

Shoulders, arms, and hands, or what is considered the upper region of the upper body, have a significant effect on how a person is perceived. Whether it's your posture or your hand and arm movement, every gesture plays a role. Some important gestures of the upper body are:

- When people raise one shoulder towards their ear, this often means they're doubtful or insecure about something. Whereas tilting your shoulder towards a romantic interest conveys that you're interested.
- The various animated gestures made through our hands are used to convey so many feelings, whether it's excitement, anger, nervousness, frustration, or disappointment. Since gestures are considered to be the most important part of body language, they should be analyzed with as much focus and importance.
- Moreover, arms tend to stiffen when people are in stressful or scary situations. Their arms lie dormant at their sides, giving them an unnatural and robotic look. Crossing the arms is done for various reasons, including protection, comfort, self-restraint,

or dislike.

- Hand displays are also signs of emotions. For instance, when a person splays out their hands on a table, it indicates an attempt at intimidation and feelings of superiority, but not exactly in a bad way.

- Hands, when placed in ready or active mode, are often done to capture the listeners' attention at important moments. Moreover, handshaking is also an essential communicator of how one feels. Tighter handshakes indicate intense emotions, whereas loose handshakes reflect the person's laziness.

The Chest

The chest is an important part of body language and plays into many communicative gestures. Moreover, how one carries themselves also helps determine their personality and current emotional wellbeing. Some traits to look out for are:

- A heaving chest combined with rapid breathing indicates anxiety, worry, concern, fear, or maybe physical exertion. However, this gesture may also be a symptom of a heart attack if observed with chest pains.

- When a person is under stress, they tend to press on their own chest with their thumb and index finger to relieve their worry. This is a pacifying gesture, and it helps soothe them.

- If a person repetitively massages their chest with their hand, it indicates concern, worry, or anxiety. If this is continued for long periods of time, it can be associated with an impending panic or anxiety attack. This behavior usually stands out because of the posture of the hand, which, instead of staying relaxed, as usual, is generally curled like a claw or rake.

- In many cultures, when people place their palms on their chests, they are considered to be speaking genuinely or telling the truth when answering a question. It can also be associated with making true promises and genuine commitments.

- People are often seen playing with the zipper of their hoodies or jackets. This is mainly associated with pacifying gestures and is done when a person feels stressed or anxious. The repetitive motion helps them relax and calm their nerves.

Legs and Feet

Legs and feet are often ignored when it comes to non-verbal communication and body language analysis. However, they are pretty much essential to conveying a message through our stance and posture. How you keep your legs when you're standing, or sitting, tells a lot about how you're feeling. Similarly, the way you move your feet also communicates your thoughts and emotions to an observer. Some of these gestures can include:

- A person who stands with their legs apart displays a territorial stance. The wider their legs are apart, the more intimidating they seem
- Keeping your legs angled is another one of your unconscious non-verbal traits – and often goes unnoticed. People often do this to have a better grasp of the conversation
- What can a person's walk tell you about their personality? If a person walks fast and has a purposeful gait, they are considered to be confident. Whereas if a person walks with a slouched or bad posture, they're considered lazy or lethargic.
- When sitting, legs held tightly together indicate insecurity or even discomfort. Whereas people sitting with their legs slightly apart are considered to be confident and easy-going. This is why it's best to have a relaxed stance with your legs slightly apart to give off a confident vibe.

Whether it's verbal or non-verbal cues, every part of our communication system has an essential role in the art of communicating. When trying to read someone, it's essential that you observe their body language and little quirks and gestures that usually go unnoticed by people because they will tell you more about the person than they ever will by themselves.

Conclusion

The world is populated by numerous living species, many of which are smart, tactical, deceptive, and intuitive. However, what makes us humans very special is that we always try to understand others. Even if we're not necessarily conscious of these efforts, we always pick up on underlying hints and messages. For instance, if you're hanging out with a friend who mentions that they haven't eaten anything since the morning, you'd probably take that as a hint that they're hungry. Understanding and analyzing the words and actions of others is vital for socialization. It enhances mutual aid, along with our survival and comfort, depending on the context and the situation.

Understanding others broadens our perspectives. It promotes the development of other intrapersonal skills like empathy, understanding and applying personal boundaries, and creating values. While understanding other people is what makes us good friends, family members, employees, and members of the community. It also helps us protect ourselves. People's actions, words, and behaviors aren't always genuine. Mastering the art of analyzing people can help us pick up on lies and deception. Understanding other people is a fundamental survival skill. That said, it's not always an easy feat.

Human beings are incredibly complicated. There are many underlying factors, including a person's feelings, thoughts, mood, past experiences, underlying trauma, illnesses, and tiredness, to account for when we're trying to understand others. We are often put off by people who get defensive or aggressive all of a sudden, not knowing that something we said may have triggered a past wound. The likelihood of us understanding others depends on our personal state as well. We are less likely to spend time understanding others when we're tired or irritable.

We can often get a sense of a person's emotions by looking out for their facial expressions, mannerisms, and general appearance. In some cases, getting grips with non-verbal cues may be challenging. Fortunately, now that you have read this book, you know everything there is to know about analyzing individuals. Putting this invaluable information into practice can help you improve your social cognition.

You are now aware of how important a person's behavior is, what it can tell you about them, and how you're feeling. Implementing this information into your daily life can help you strengthen your relationships with others. Understanding how other people feel and why they act the way they do can help you build tighter bonds with those around you. The best thing about learning to analyze people is that it creates a sense of intimacy between you and others without forcing you to risk your own well-being and protection. We must let our guard down to get intimate with the people we love. Doing so leaves us vulnerable to their lies, deception, and manipulative tactics. This is why many people enforce very strict boundaries and avoid opening up to others easily. Luckily, when you have high social cognition, you are less likely to fall into these traps.

Here's another book by Andy Gardner that you might like

Free Bonus from Andy Gardner

Hi!

My name is Andy Gardner, and first off, I want to THANK YOU for reading my book.

Now you have a chance to join my exclusive email list related to human psychology and self-development so you can get the ebook below for free as well as the potential to get more ebooks for free! Simply click the link below to join.

P.S. Remember that it's 100% free to join the list.

Access your free bonuses here:
https://livetolearn.lpages.co/andy-gardner-communication-skills-paperback/

References

What are communication skills? Types and importance of communication skillsASM IBMR

7 types of communication skills - verbal, non-verbal. (2022, February 2). CourseMentorTM. https://coursementor.com/blog/types-of-communication-skills/

American English Skills Development Center. (2022, April 5). What are the benefits of effective communication skills. Linkedin.com. https://www.linkedin.com/pulse/what-benefits-effective-communication-/?trk=organization-update-content_share-article

CLIMB Professional Development, & Training. (2019, July 9). The 7 benefits of effective communication in personal and professional settings. Pcc.edu. https://climb.pcc.edu/blog/the-7-benefits-of-effective-communication-in-personal-and-professional-settings

Five types of communication. (2018, July 12). Graduate College of Drexel University. https://drexel.edu/graduatecollege/professional-development/blog/2018/July/Five-types-of-communication/

Caputa, P. (2018, April 23). Active listening in sales: The ultimate guide. HubSpot. https://blog.hubspot.com/sales/active-listening-guide

Ld, C. (2012, May 3). Successful communication is a two way street. Catalyst Learning & Development. https://cbduk.wordpress.com/2012/05/03/successful-communication-is-a-two-way-street/

Saha, S. (n.d.). Active listening: How important this skill is in mentoring? Mentoringcomplete.com

Carpenter, D. (2015, November 25). 3 ways to build real empathy for others in your life. Verywell Mind. https://www.verywellmind.com/how-to-develop-empathy-in-relationships-1717547

Cherry, K. (2006, September 8). What is emotional intelligence? Verywell Mind. https://www.verywellmind.com/what-is-emotional-intelligence-2795423

Cherry, K. (2015, January 5). What is empathy? Verywell Mind. https://www.verywellmind.com/what-is-empathy-2795562

Dial, M. (2019, July 30). Five everyday exercises for building empathy. INSEAD Knowledge. https://knowledge.insead.edu/career/five-everyday-exercises-building-empathy

In Professional Development. (2022, April 1). 3 ways Emotional Intelligence will improve your communication. Inpd.co.uk. https://www.inpd.co.uk/blog/3-ways-emotional-intelligence-will-improve-your-communication?hs_amp=true

Jacobson, S. (2016, May 5). Emotional awareness - what it is and why you need it. Harley TherapyTM Blog; Harley Therapy. https://www.harleytherapy.co.uk/counselling/emotional-awareness.htm

Schmitz, T. (2016, June 3). The importance of emotional awareness in communication. The Conover Company. https://www.conovercompany.com/the-importance-of-emotional-awareness-in-communication/

Turning Point Resolutions Inc. (2021, May 21). 10 tips for improving your nonverbal communication. Turning Point Resolutions Inc. https://turningpointresolutions.com/10-tips-for-improving-your-nonverbal-communication/

Clear, J. (2013, July 25). How to be confident and reduce stress in 2 minutes per day. James Clear. https://jamesclear.com/body-language-how-to-be-confident

Cherry, K. (2017, July 27). Understanding body language and facial expressions. Verywell Mind. https://www.verywellmind.com/understand-body-language-and-facial-expressions-4147228

Spence, J. (2020, February 18). Nonverbal communication: How body language & nonverbal cues are key. Lifesize. https://www.lifesize.com/en/blog/speaking-without-words/

Forbes Coaches Council. (2018, October 18). 11 nonverbal ways to express empathy and camaraderie with your team. Forbes. https://www.forbes.com/sites/forbescoachescouncil/2018/10/18/11-nonverbal-ways-to-express-empathy-and-camaraderie-with-your-team/?sh=7d8033605151

Barnum, C., & Wolniansky, N. (1989, June). Taking cues from body language. Management Review, 78, 59+. https://go.gale.com/ps/i.do?id=GALE%7CA7640467&sid=googleScholar&v=2.1&it=r&linkaccess=abs&issn=00251895&p=AONE&sw=w&userGroupName=anon%7E16cb9f2b

Canada, A. (2019, April 17). Effective Communication - Improving your Social Skills. Anxiety Canada. https://www.anxietycanada.com/articles/effective-communication-improving-your-social-skills/

Waters, S. (n.d.). How to make a good first impression: Expert tips and tricks. Betterup.com. https://www.betterup.com/blog/how-to-make-a-good-first-impression

Young Entrepreneur Council. (2019, April 3). 11 tips for making A great first impression with new clients. Forbes. https://www.forbes.com/sites/theyec/2019/04/03/11-tips-for-making-a-great-first-impression-with-potential-new-clients/?sh=6b0ce195bd4f

How to make a good first impression: 7 tips that really work. (2020, November 25). ZenBusiness Inc. https://www.zenbusiness.com/blog/seven-tips/

Svitorka, T. (2019, July 28). 6 tips How to master small talk and never feel awkward again. Tomas Svitorka - London Life Coach. https://tomassvitorka.com/master-small-talk/

6 tips to master small talk. (2021, February 18). Make Me Better. https://www.makemebetter.net/6-tips-to-master-small-talk/

Viktor Sander B. Sc., B. A., Morin, D. A., & Ashfield, C. (2020, October 22). How to make conversation as an introvert. SocialSelf. https://socialself.com/blog/make-conversation-introvert/

Thorp, T. (2020, March 16). 10 ways to deepen your connections with others. Chopra. https://chopra.com/articles/10-ways-to-deepen-your-connections-with-others

Mokhtar, N. H., Halim, M. F. A., & Kamarulzaman, S. Z. S. (2011). The effectiveness of storytelling in enhancing communicative skills. Procedia, Social and Behavioral Sciences, 18, 163–169. https://doi.org/10.1016/j.sbspro.2011.05.024

Nandy, P. (2017, March 22). 5 ways storytelling can be used to improve communication. Com.au. https://www.insidehr.com.au/how-top-companies-use-storytelling-to-drive-results/

Parekh, D. (2019, October 14). Communicate your Point of View through storytelling. Forbes. https://www.forbes.com/sites/forbescoachescouncil/2019/10/14/communicate-your-point-of-view-through-storytelling/?sh=54821be541bf

Sundin, A., Andersson, K., & Watt, R. (2018). Rethinking communication: integrating storytelling for increased stakeholder engagement in environmental evidence synthesis. Environmental Evidence, 7(1), 1–6. https://doi.org/10.1186/s13750-018-0116-4

Woodget, M. (2022, February 10). The importance of storytelling. Go Narrative! https://www.gonarrative.com/blog/2022/2/10/the-importance-of-storytelling

Ahmed, A. (2010, July 30). Effective Group Communication Processes. Small Business - Chron.com; Chron.com. https://smallbusiness.chron.com/effective-group-communication-processes-3187.html

Festinger, L., & Thibaut, J. (1951). Interpersonal communication in small groups. Journal of Abnormal Psychology, 46(1), 92–99. https://doi.org/10.1037/h0054899

Gail, C. (n.d.). Team Communication: Effective Group Collaboration & Teamwork. Crystalknows.com. https://www.crystalknows.com/blog/team-communication

Quinn, J. (2020, November 3). How much of communication is nonverbal? The University of Texas Permian Basin | UTPB; The University of Texas Permian Basin. https://online.utpb.edu/about-us/articles/communication/how-much-of-communication-is-nonverbal/

8 fears of public speaking and how to overcome them. (2016, November 17). Elaine Powell website: https://elainepowell.com/all-posts/8-fears-of-public-speaking-and-how-to-overcome-them/

A guide to confidence in public speaking. (2021, April 26). Throughline Group website: https://www.throughlinegroup.com/resources/confidence-in-public-speaking/

Brown, M. (2011, April 18). What Are the Problems of Public Speaking? Pen and the Pad website: https://penandthepad.com/info-8247710-problems-public-speaking.html

Expert Panel®. (2021, July 15). How to fix 14 public speaking issues professionals commonly overlook. Forbes website: https://www.forbes.com/sites/forbescoachescouncil/2021/07/15/how-to-fix-14-public-speaking-issues-professionals-commonly-overlook/?sh=43c8a9b04c14

Genard, G. (n.d.). 10 fast and effective ways to overcome stage fright. Genardmethod.com website: https://www.genardmethod.com/blog/10-fast-and-effective-ways-to-overcome-stage-fright

LaDouceur, P. (n.d.). What we fear more than death. Mentalhelp.net website: https://www.mentalhelp.net/blogs/what-we-fear-more-than-death/

Cooke, E. (2012, January 15). How narratives can aid memory. The Guardian. https://www.theguardian.com/lifeandstyle/2012/jan/15/story-lines-facts

Sheeran, P. (2002). Intention—behavior relations: A conceptual and empirical review. European Review of Social Psychology, 12(1), 1–36. https://doi.org/10.1080/14792772143000003

Spence, G. (1996). How to argue and win every time, at home, at work, in court, everywhere, every day. Sidgwick & Jackson.

Splitter, J., & Danielle Murphy, L. (n.d.). How to have healthier arguments. Everydayhealth.com. https://www.everydayhealth.com/emotional-health/how-to-have-healthier-arguments-according-to-psychologists/

Stone, D. (1999). Difficult Conversations: How to Discuss what Matters Most. Michael Joseph.

The link and story methods. (n.d.). Mindtools.com. https://www.mindtools.com/pages/article/newTIM_01.htm

Van Edwards, V. (2020, August 27). 62 ways to politely end a conversation in ANY situation. Science of People. https://www.scienceofpeople.com/end-conversation/

Miller, K. (2021, November 18). 12 tips for how to end a conversation instead of dying a thousand deaths in moments of awkward silence. Well+Good. https://www.wellandgood.com/how-to-end-conversation/

Jones, B. (2017, June 1). How to end a conversation: Strategies and expressions you can use. Get More Vocab; Bradford Jones. https://getmorevocab.com/strategies-expressions-ending-conversation/

Top 5 communication skills and how to improve them. (2022, February 22). Haiilo. https://haiilo.com/blog/top-5-communication-skills-and-how-to-improve-them/

Biehl, M., Matsumoto, D., Ekman, P., Hearn, V., Heider, K., Kudoh, T., & Ton, V. (1997). Journal of Non-verbal Behavior, 21(1), 3–21. https://doi.org/10.1023/a:1024902500935

Carroll, L., & Gilroy, P. J. (2002). Role of appearance and non-verbal behaviors in the perception of sexual orientation among lesbians and gay men. Psychological Reports, 91(1), 115–122. https://doi.org/10.2466/pr0.2002.91.1.115

Cherry, K. (2005, November 23). Color psychology: Does it affect how you feel? Verywell Mind. https://www.verywellmind.com/color-psychology-2795824

Cherry, K. (2013, October 21). Are our emotional expressions universal? Verywell Mind. https://www.verywellmind.com/the-expression-of-emotion-2795180

Cowen, A. S., Keltner, D., Schroff, F., Jou, B., Adam, H., & Prasad, G. (2021). Sixteen facial expressions occur in similar contexts worldwide. Nature, 589(7841), 251–257. https://doi.org/10.1038/s41586-020-3037-7

D'Agostino, T. A., & Bylund, C. L. (2014). Non-verbal accommodation in health care communication. Health Communication, 29(6), 563–573. https://doi.org/10.1080/10410236.2013.783773

Eisenbarth, H., & Alpers, G. W. (2011). Happy mouth and sad eyes: Scanning emotional facial expressions. Emotion (Washington, D.C.), 11(4), 860–865. https://doi.org/10.1037/a0022758

Goldin-Meadow, S. (2014). How gesture works to change our minds. Trends in Neuroscience and Education, 3(1), 4–6. https://doi.org/10.1016/j.tine.2014.01.002

Iwasaki, M., & Noguchi, Y. (2016). Hiding true emotions: micro-expressions in eyes retrospectively concealed by mouth movements. Scientific Reports, 6(1), 22049. https://doi.org/10.1038/srep22049

Jiang, J., Borowiak, K., Tudge, L., Otto, C., & von Kriegstein, K. (2016). Neural mechanisms of eye contact when listening to another person talking. Social Cognitive and Affective Neuroscience, nsw127. https://doi.org/10.1093/scan/nsw127

McCall, C., & Singer, T. (2015). Facing off with unfair others: introducing proxemic imaging as an implicit measure of approach and avoidance during social interaction. PloS One, 10(2), e0117532. https://doi.org/10.1371/journal.pone.0117532

Oh Kruzic, C., Kruzic, D., Herrera, F., & Bailenson, J. (2020). Facial expressions contribute more than body movements to conversational outcomes in avatar-mediated virtual environments. Scientific Reports, 10(1), 20626. https://doi.org/10.1038/s41598-020-76672-4

Romig, J. (n.d.). Non-verbal communication –. Listen Like a Lawyer. Retrieved July 29, 2022, from https://listenlikealawyer.com/tag/non-verbal-communication/

Sokolov, A. A., Krüger, S., Enck, P., Krägeloh-Mann, I., & Pavlova, M. A. (2011). Gender affects body language reading. Frontiers in Psychology, 2, 16. https://doi.org/10.3389/fpsyg.2011.00016

Song, J., Wang, L., & Wang, W. (2012). Eyebrow segmentation based on binary edge image. In Lecture Notes in Computer Science (pp. 350–356). Springer Berlin Heidelberg.

Teigen, K. H. (2008). Is a sigh "just a sigh"? Sighs as emotional signals and responses to a difficult task: Is a sigh "just a sigh"? Scandinavian Journal of Psychology, 49(1), 49–57. https://doi.org/10.1111/j.1467-9450.2007.00599.x

www.ingramcontent.com/pod-product-compliance
Lightning Source LLC
Chambersburg PA
CBHW070327010526
44107CB00004B/438